"*VALOR—A Gathering of Eagles* will pull at your heart strings and renew your passion for everything that is good and right as you relive the exploits of great American heroes. It puts new meaning to the words courage, honor, sacrifice, and faith in God. You will be inspired to live above the common level of life...like those who risked it all for their buddies, their units, and their country."

MG Robert VanAntwerp, U.S. Army
President, Officer Christian Fellowship

"'Be strong and courageous, I'll never leave you or forsake you' (Joshua 1:19). Courage, valor, faith, and hope are reflected in the lives of so many of these men who received the Medal of Honor. *VALOR—A Gathering of Eagles* encourages all of us to be people of conviction and character."

Brig Gen Dick Abel, USAF (Ret.)
Military Ministry, Campus Crusade for Christ

"America needs warriors. This book is the story of some who have led the way and now share their faith and wisdom in a candid way. It will encourage and inspire the reader."

MG William Boykin
United States Army

"I know Colonel Bernie Fisher and the faith he exercised on March 10, 1966. Prayer and faith were the basis of his decision and his courage to rescue Jump Meyers from the clutches of the NVA after crash landing at a contested jungle airstrip in Vietnam. Jim Coy's book, *VALOR—A Gathering of Eagles,* is the testimony of Bernie and many other Medal of Honor recipients' faith in God."

Lt Gen Bruce Fister, USAF (Ret.)
Executive Director, Officer Christian Fellowship

"I know of no other character trait valued more than courage. It is the one element that takes ordinary people and transforms them—and everyone around them. In *VALOR—A Gathering of Eagles,* Colonel Jim Coy draws out the life lessons of those who have been awarded our highest honor for courage."

Maj Gen Jerry White, USAF (Ret.)
President, The Navigators

"The men depicted in *VALOR—A Gathering of Eagles*, represent America's best. They are men with character and courage who sacrificed without question for the United States and for people they did not know in faraway places. Their deeds speak volumes as they provide insight for all. Individuals like these will continue to keep America the land of the free for the future."

GEN John Tilelli, USA (Ret.)
Former Commanding General, UN and US Forces - Korea

"The creature seeks the Creator. To help each other in the quest, our lives are meant to point to Him. But a few people, capable of heroic virtue, draw bold blue arrows on the map of our lives. This book is about men such as these."

VADM Art Cebrowski, USN (Ret.)
Former President, U.S. Naval War College

"The inspirational stories in *VALOR—A Gathering of Eagles* are, in themselves, an inspiration. These heroes stand for duty, honor, and country, but they stand for much more than that. Rather, they stand for all that is right, good, and decent. Further, they serve as a reminder that all of our hopes and dreams, yours and mine, collectively are entrusted to the domain of the soldier, the airman, the Marine, and to all those who serve in uniform. They have never failed us and I suggest that they never shall...must reading for all."

GEN John Coburn, USA (Ret.)
Former Commander, U.S. Army Materiel Command

"As Joshua was exhorted to 'be strong and courageous' on the eve of the battle of Jericho, so have men in each generation been called to extraordinary bravery in combat and sought the same Source of strength as Joshua. This book chronicles the experiences and insights of Americans whose courageous service under fire has been recognized by the nation's highest decoration—the Medal of Honor. They have earned the right to be heard, and I recommend it highly."

VADM J. Scott Redd, USN (Ret.)
Founder and former Commander, U.S. FIFTH Fleet

VALOR
A Gathering of Eagles

VALOR
A Gathering of Eagles

COL Jimmie Dean Coy (Ret.)

VALOR—A Gathering of Eagles

*The publisher wishes to thank the Congressional Medal of Honor Society
for the information obtained at their website and used both in the citations and in the sidebars and also for their valuable help by providing
photographs. Their website is: www.cmohs.org and it contains a myriad
of information about the Medal of Honor and its recipients.*

*The official citations are included as issued with only minor grammati-
cal corrections. Military abbreviations and numerical designations were
kept intact.*

ISBN: 1-58169-111-4
For Worldwide Distribution
Printed in the U.S.A.

Evergreen Press
P.O. Box 191540 • Mobile, AL 36619
800-367-8203

TABLE OF CONTENTS

DEDICATION

To those who serve, to those who have served and especially to those who are and were willing to lay down their life for another.

"Greater love hath no man than this, that a man lay down his life for his friends" (John 15:13).

ACKNOWLEDGMENTS

First, I must thank every recipient of the Medal of Honor for what they did and are still doing for freedom. I want to thank every individual who was willing to offer their advice for this book. The wisdom given is from the hearts of patriots.

SPECIAL THANKS

To my mother and father, who always demonstrated unconditional love for each other and for their children. For their constant example of honesty, work ethic, and dedication to faith and family.

To my brothers, both career military sergeants, both heroes. Thanks for the advice you gave me so many years ago: "Don't just be a doctor that wears a uniform, be a soldier first, and also be a good doctor." Together we served the nation for a total 92 years in Army green.

To my wife, Vicki (You are my life!), and my children, Tim, Tricia, and Joshua. Thank you for your love, even when I could or should have been a better husband and father.

To my publisher, Evergreen Press. Brian, you had an understanding of the importance of the project from our first discussion. Thanks!

Finally, and most importantly, I want to thank God for blessing and allowing me to work on this project and for His words of direction and encouragement in Joshua 24:15, "As for me and my house we will serve the Lord."

INTRODUCTION

When I first began gathering advice for life from men who were recipients of the Medal of Honor, I felt blessed to be able to come to know these American heroes! They are the bravest of the brave. As I developed friendships with many of these men over the years, I was impressed with the humility, honesty, and love of nation of every one of them. I salute these heroes!

I asked these men: "What is your creed or code of conduct for life?" or "What is your motto for life?" I also asked them: "How do you move from success to significance?"

The advice they offer is the same advice that they would give to their children or grandchildren, but in this case the advice is for our future leaders, for the young men and women of America.

The book includes advice for life from each individual followed by their Medal of Honor citation. Eleven of the men have also offered an inspirational story for the book. They are: Nick Bacon, Gary Beikirch, Pat Brady, Charles Coolidge, Desmond Doss, Walter Ehlers, Joe Foss, "Rudy" Hernandez, Bob Maxwell, Mitch Paige, and Leo Thorsness. These eleven men are all featured in the Family Net video: VALOR. (See page 302 for how to order.)

—*Colonel Jim Coy (Ret.)*

THE MEDAL OF HONOR

Established by Act of Congress in 1862, it is the highest and most rarely awarded decoration conferred by the United States. The deed for which the Medal of Honor is awarded must have been one of personal bravery or self-sacrifice so conspicuous as to clearly distinguish the individual for gallantry and intrepidity above his comrades and must have involved risk of life. Incontestable proof of the performance of the service will be exacted on the standard of extraordinary merit.

Three questions were asked
of men who had been awarded
the Medal of Honor:

What is your creed or code of conduct for life?

How do you move from success to significance?

*What is your advice for life for our nation's
future leaders?*

Each response is followed by the official citation
detailing the acts of bravery for which they were
awarded the Medal of Honor.

Webster Anderson
U.S. Army • Vietnam

"My creed for a successful life is to put God first, my country next, and then myself. I would offer this advice to young people: be honest, loyal, and most of all, have self-respect. These values are dear to me because they are the basis of America and our way of life."

Rank and organization
Sergeant First Class, U.S. Army, Battery A, 2d Battalion, 320th Field Artillery, 101st Airborne Infantry Division (Airmobile).
Place and date:
Tam Ky, Republic of Vietnam, 15 October 1967.

CITATION

Sfc. Anderson (then S/Sgt.), distinguished himself by conspicuous gallantry and intrepidity in action while serving as chief of section in Battery A, against a hostile force.

During the early morning hours Battery A's defensive position was attacked by a determined North Vietnamese Army infantry unit supported by heavy mortar, recoilless rifle, rocket propelled grenade and automatic weapon fire. The initial enemy onslaught breached the battery defensive perimeter. Sfc. Anderson, with complete disregard for his personal safety, mounted the exposed parapet of his howitzer position and became the mainstay of the defense of the battery position. Sfc. Anderson directed devastating direct howitzer fire on the assaulting enemy while providing rifle and grenade defensive fire against enemy soldiers attempting to overrun his gun section position.

While protecting his crew and directing their fire against the enemy from his exposed position, 2 enemy grenades exploded at his feet, knocking him down and severely wounding him in the legs. Despite the excruciating pain and though not able to stand, Sfc. Anderson valorously propped himself on the parapet and continued to direct howitzer fire upon the closing enemy and to encourage his men to fight on. Seeing an enemy grenade land within the gun pit near a wounded member of his gun crew, Sfc. Anderson, heedless of his own safety, seized the grenade and attempted to throw it over the parapet to save his men. As the grenade was thrown from the position, it exploded and Sfc. Anderson was again grievously wounded. Although only partially conscious and severely wounded, Sfc. Anderson refused medical evacuation and continued to encourage his men in the defense of the position.

Sfc. Anderson, by his inspirational leadership, professionalism, devotion to duty, and complete disregard for his welfare, was able to maintain the defense of his section position and to defeat a determined attack. Sfc. Anderson's gallantry and extraordinary heroism at the risk of his life above and beyond the call of duty are in the highest traditions of the military service and reflect great credit upon himself, his unit, and the U.S. Army.

John P. Baca
U.S. Army • Vietnam

"When Mother Teresa of Calcutta received the Nobel Peace Prize she said, 'We can do no great things, only small things through great love.' We often surprise ourselves by our response to situations and events that occur during our lives. In life we find ourselves in a wide variety of circumstances, some not by choice.

"It is true that our imagination is greater, even more powerful, than knowledge. We must realize there is a Power within each of us that can allow us to embrace hardship, endure pain, and be accepting of difficult and even impossible circumstances.

"The greatest, most traumatic (yet peaceful) moments in my life happened when I was wounded and severely injured in Vietnam. Those moments were peaceful because I was held, embraced, and loved by my guardian angel. I realized that my death, if it were to happen, would have been the beginning of an eternal life.

"We must believe in a spiritual power in the universe, and that it is a part of each of us. That power desires to love others and all living things within our own world. To plant a seed or to plant a garden is to believe in tomorrow!

"One additional quote that I really like is also by Mother Teresa: 'We are all pencils in the hand of God.' With that quote, my advice to young men and women is to encourage you to keep your pencil sharpened and ready to use."

Rank and organization
Specialist Fourth Class, U.S. Army, Company D,
1st Battalion, 12th Cavalry, 1st Cavalry Division.
Place and date
Phuoc Long Province, Republic of Vietnam, 10 February 1970.

CITATION

For conspicuous gallantry and intrepidity in action at the risk of his life above and beyond the call of duty. Sp4c. Baca, Company D, distinguished himself while serving on a recoilless rifle team during a night ambush mission

A platoon from his company was sent to investigate the detonation of an automatic ambush device forward of his unit's main position and soon came under intense enemy fire from concealed positions along the trail. Hearing the heavy firing from the platoon position and realizing that his recoilless rifle team could assist the members of the besieged patrol, Sp4c. Baca led his team through the hail of enemy fire to a firing position within the patrol's defensive perimeter. As they prepared to engage the enemy, a fragmentation grenade was thrown into the midst of the patrol. Fully aware of the danger to his comrades, Sp4c. Baca unhesitatingly, and with complete disregard for his own safety, covered the grenade with his steel helmet and fell on it as the grenade exploded, thereby absorbing the lethal fragments and concussion with his body.

His gallant action and total disregard for his personal well-being directly saved 8 men from certain serious injury or death. The extraordinary courage and selflessness displayed by Sp4c. Baca, at the risk of his life, are in the highest traditions of the military service and reflect great credit on him, his unit, and the U.S. Army.

First Sergeant Nicky D. Bacon
U.S. Army (Ret.) • Vietnam

"In combat, my faith in God grew as did my respect for the word 'honor.' I wish I could sit down at a campfire with all of our nation's children, and they would listen to my words of advice. They are simple words: No one is perfect, everyone fails and often comes a little short of what we expect of ourselves.

"I have traveled the world and have seen many places and different races of people. I trained years for war and fought in the dark jungles of Vietnam. Yet, I know so little, I feel so small. I have searched for strength and found weakness. I have found the true and everlasting strength only through faith in my God. I have found that, through prayer, I am a giant of power and ability. But faith is not something that just happens, you must develop it. With faith you can move a mountain, keep a family together, help a friend, or even win a war.

"If you desire spiritual greatness, you must humble yourself, set aside all your human pride, study the Word of God, and always be in prayer."

Rank and Organization
Staff Sergeant, U.S. Army, Company B, 4th Battalion,
21st Infantry, 11th Infantry Brigade, Americal Division.
Place and date
West of Tam Ky, Republic of Vietnam, 8/26/68.

CITATION

For conspicuous gallantry and intrepidity in action at the risk of his life above and beyond the call of duty. S/Sgt. Bacon distinguished himself while serving as a squad leader with the 1st Platoon, Company B, during an operation west of Tam Ky.

When Company B came under fire from an enemy bunker line to the front, S/Sgt. Bacon quickly organized his men and led them forward in an assault. He advanced on a hostile bunker and destroyed it with grenades. As he did so, several fellow soldiers including the 1st Platoon leader, were struck by machine gun fire and fell wounded in an exposed position forward of the rest of the platoon. S/Sgt. Bacon immediately assumed command of the platoon and assaulted the hostile gun position, finally killing the enemy gun . crew in a single-handed effort.

When the 3d Platoon moved to S/Sgt. Bacon's location, its leader was also wounded. Without hesitation, S/Sgt. Bacon took charge of the additional platoon and continued the fight. In the ensuing action, he personally killed 4 more enemy soldiers and silenced an antitank weapon.

Under his leadership and example, the members of both platoons accepted his authority without question. Continuing to ignore the intense hostile fire, he climbed up on the exposed deck of a tank and directed fire into the enemy position while several wounded men were evacuated.

As a result of S/Sgt. Bacon's extraordinary efforts, his company was able to move forward, eliminate the enemy positions, and rescue the men trapped at the front. S/Sgt. Bacon's bravery at the risk of his life was in the highest traditions of the military service and reflects great credit upon himself, his unit, and the U.S. Army.

NO GREATER GIFT—
A HERO'S HEART

I was born in Caraway, Arkansas—a small farming community in northeast Arkansas. Most of my family members and friends were from the same economically depressed surroundings. Cotton was the king and when poor crop prices hit us hard, bad times got worse. The one thing I remember most about my younger years in the cotton fields was that although we were poor and times were hard, people were most always cheerful, trusted in God, and loved one another.

My childhood experience in hardship and my close association with a group of people who had great values and steadfast faith helped me develop a trust in God that far exceeded any faith in my own abilities. This same faith gave me confidence to overcome obstacles in life, in combat, in my profession as a soldier, and in the other difficulties that I would face.

I survived two tours in the jungles of Vietnam with combat infantry units. I have seen many great men make sacrifices to save others—men willing to die for their friends. It takes more than just love for your country or patriotism to have great courage. It takes a hero's heart, that is, a personal love for those around you because you know they would do the same for you.

On the 26th of August, 1968, while serving with B company, the 11th Light Infantry Brigade of the Americal Division, we came under heavy fire from an enemy bunker in an area near Tam Ky. We were led by a great commander and friend, Captain Treadwell, ("Big T"). Many great Americans were struck down that day: some were wounded; some died. Many were struck down trying to help me...and they called me a hero! As always during the battle, I prayed as often as possible while dodging bullets, rocket fire, and hand grenades. Why God lets some of us live and others die I will never know, but I do know this: A man can live a lifetime helping others, but no one can give more in a lifetime than my friends gave in just one moment of time.

Life and death are as close as dark and light at early dawn. We do have a purpose in life; God has designed a plan for each of us to fulfill. We can only trust in His power and greatness, and if we continue to march forward in faith, we can finish the race set before us.
—*Nick Bacon*

Psalm 23

The LORD is my shepherd; I shall not want.

He maketh me to lie down in green pastures: he leadeth me beside the still waters.

He restoreth my soul: he leadeth me in the paths of righteousness for his name's sake.

Yea, though I walk through the valley of the shadow of death, I will fear no evil: for thou art with me; thy rod and thy staff they comfort me.

Thou preparest a table before me in the presence of mine enemies: thou anointest my head with oil; my cup runneth over.

Surely goodness and mercy shall follow me all the days of my life: and I will dwell in the house of the LORD for ever.

Master Sergeant John F. Baker
U.S. Army (Ret.) • Vietnam

"My advice to young men and women, what some might call a creed or motto for life is: Never give up. Stand up for what you believe in and what is right. Always be honest. My thoughts about success and significance are: Have faith and trust in God."

Sergeant (then Pfc.), U.S. Army, Company A,
2d Battalion, 27th Infantry, 25th Infantry Division.
Place and date
Republic of Vietnam, 5 November 1966.

CITATION

For conspicuous gallantry and intrepidity in action at the risk of his life above and beyond the call of duty.

En route to assist another unit that was engaged with the enemy, Company A came under intense enemy fire, and the lead man was killed instantly. Sgt. Baker immediately moved to the head of the column and together with another soldier knocked out 2 enemy bunkers. When his comrade was mortally wounded, Sgt. Baker, spotting 4 Viet Cong snipers, killed all of them, evacuated the fallen soldier, and returned to lead repeated assaults against the enemy positions, killing several more Viet Cong.

Moving to attack 2 additional enemy bunkers, he and another soldier drew intense enemy fire, and Sgt. Baker was blown from his feet by an enemy grenade. He quickly recovered and single-handedly destroyed 1 bunker before the other soldier was wounded. Seizing his fallen comrade's machine gun, Sgt. Baker charged through the deadly fusillade to silence the other bunker. He evacuated his comrade, replenished his ammunition, and returned to the forefront to brave the enemy fire and continue the fight. When the forward element was ordered to withdraw, he carried 1 wounded man to the rear. As he returned to evacuate another soldier, he was taken under fire by snipers but raced beyond the friendly troops to attack and kill the snipers. After evacuating the wounded man, he returned to cover the deployment of the unit. His ammunition now exhausted, he dragged 2 more of his fallen comrades to the rear.

Sgt. Baker's selfless heroism, indomitable fighting spirit, and extraordinary gallantry were directly responsible for saving the lives of several of his comrades, and inflicting serious damage on the enemy. His acts were in keeping with the highest traditions of the U.S. Army and reflect great credit upon himself and the Armed Forces of his country.

First Lieutenant Vernon J. Baker
U.S. Army (Ret.) • WWII

"The story of my life can be found in my autobiography enti-
tled *Lasting Valor.* I was orphaned at the age of four and was raised
in Wyoming by my grandparents in a town with just a dozen other
black families. I spent two years at Father Flanagan's Boys Home in
Omaha, Nebraska, and graduated from high school in Iowa.

"I joined the Army and served with one of the few all-black regiments to see combat in World War II. I remained in the Army and
became one of the first blacks to command an all-white company.
Along the way I joined the Airborne and made my last jump at age
forty-eight. After retiring from the Army, I spent nearly twenty years
working for the Red Cross.

"After years of trying to forget, of regretting many deaths, I
have been handed the hero's mantle. I wear it uneasily. People have
considerable expectations of heroes. We are not to falter in the spot-
light; we are not to have made many mistakes in the past.

"The advice that I would offer I learned from my grandfather.
He was a quiet, good, gentle man who taught me to keep cool, to
respect everyone no matter how they treated me. I try to evaluate
people the way I want them to evaluate me."

CITATION

For extraordinary heroism in action on 5 and 6 April 1945, near Viareggio, Italy. Then Second Lieutenant Baker demonstrated outstanding courage and leadership in destroying enemy installations, personnel, and equipment during his company's attack against a strongly entrenched enemy in mountainous terrain.

When his company was stopped by the concentration of fire from several machine gun emplacements, he crawled to one position and destroyed it, killing three Germans. Continuing forward, he attacked an enemy observation post and killed two occupants. With the aid of one of his men, Lieutenant Baker attacked two more machine gun nests, killing or wounding the four enemy soldiers occupying these positions. He then covered the evacuation of the wounded personnel of his company by occupying an exposed position and drawing the enemy's fire. On the following night, Lieutenant Baker voluntarily led a battalion advance through enemy mine fields and heavy fire toward the division objective.

Second Lieutenant Baker's fighting spirit and daring leadership were an inspiration to his men and exemplify the highest traditions of the Armed Forces.

Colonel Donald E. Ballard
U.S. Army National Guard (Ret.) • Vietnam

*(Received the Medal of Honor as a Navy
Corpsman with the U.S. Marine Corps)*

"Success' worst enemy is complacency. Get involved and stop whining.

"Winning is a habit. So is losing. We must develop the right habits to increase the chance that we will lead a good life. We must put the important things first. God has given us life, and we must develop opportunities in order to live a life of abundance. We must be proactive by getting involved in our communities and help to inspire the youth of America to choose the right path.

"We need to develop our listening skills and seek to understand before we expect to be understood. We need to 'sharpen our saw' and treat other people with a win-win attitude.

"There are a lot of great books available to us. The two that have made the greatest impact on my success are: 1) the Bible and 2) Dr. Stephen Covey's book: *7 Habits of Highly Effective People*.

"The acronym B.I.B.L.E. represents Basic Instruction Before Leaving Earth.

"Let go and let God."

Rank and organization
Hospital Corpsman Second Class, U.S. Navy, Company M,
3d Battalion, 4th Marines, 3d Marine Division.
Place and date
Quang Tri Province, Republic of Vietnam, 16 May 1968.

CITATION

For conspicuous gallantry and intrepidity at the risk of his life and beyond the call of duty while serving as a HC2c. with Company M, in connection with operations against enemy aggressor forces.

During the afternoon hours, Company M was moving to join the remainder of the 3d Battalion in Quang Tri Province. After treating and evacuating 2 heat casualties, HC2c. Ballard was returning to his platoon from the evacuation landing zone when the company was ambushed by a North Vietnamese Army unit, employing automatic weapons and mortars, and sustained numerous casualties. Observing a wounded marine, HC2c. Ballard unhesitatingly moved across the fire-swept terrain to the injured man and swiftly rendered medical assistance to his comrade. HC2c. Ballard then directed 4 marines to carry the casualty to a position of relative safety. As the 4 men prepared to move the wounded marine, an enemy soldier suddenly left his concealed position and, after hurling a hand grenade which landed near the casualty, commenced firing upon the small group of men. Instantly shouting a warning to the marines, HC2c. Ballard fearlessly threw himself upon the lethal explosive device to protect his comrades from the deadly blast. When the grenade failed to detonate, he calmly arose from his dangerous position and resolutely continued his determined efforts in treating other marine casualties.

HC2c. Ballard's heroic actions and selfless concern for the welfare of his companions served to inspire all who observed him and prevented possible injury or death to his fellow marines. His courage, daring initiative, and unwavering devotion to duty in the face of extreme personal danger, sustain and enhance the finest traditions of the U.S. Naval Service.

Colonel Van T. Barfoot
U.S. Army (Ret.) • WWII

"I was raised in a large family on our farm in rural Leake County, Mississippi. It was during the period of America's Great Depression, after WWI and through the 1930s. We had no real wealth; however, we lived a comfortable life on the farm. My father was a farmer and my mother worked in the home, spending much of her time caring for our family of nine children. Our home was a Christian home where mother was the spiritual leader. Through her evening Bible readings and prayer with the family, she taught us that God would bless those who love and put their trust in Him. My father was a hard-working man who devoted his life to providing for his family during a difficult economic period in American history. He was completely honest and taught the family to be honest and fair when dealing with others. He loved his family, God, and country. Through his work and deeds, he taught these principles to the family.

"All the children of the family attended school at a consolidated school (both elementary and high school), which was two miles from our home. After the first school period, those who had reached the teenage years worked on the farm, helping with whatever chores there were to do. Through this, children learned the value of work and responsibility to help others."

"My advice is do what you know is right and do not do what you know is not right. Be totally honest. Hard work is important. Accept responsibility to help others. I would also encourage every young man and woman to pursue their education, to learn as much as they can."

———◆◆◆———

Rank and organization
Second Lieutenant, U.S. Army, 157th Infantry, 45th Infantry Div.
Place and date
Near Carano, Italy, 23 May 1944.

CITATION

For conspicuous gallantry and intrepidity at the risk of life above and beyond the call of duty on 23 May 1944, near Carano, Italy.

With his platoon heavily engaged during an assault against forces well entrenched on commanding ground, 2d Lt. Barfoot (then Tech. Sgt.) moved off alone upon the enemy left flank. He crawled to the proximity of 1 machinegun nest and made a direct hit on it with a hand grenade, killing 2 and wounding 3 Germans. He continued along the German defense line to another machinegun emplacement, and with his tommygun killed 2 and captured 3 soldiers. Members of another enemy machinegun crew then abandoned their position and gave themselves up to Sgt. Barfoot. Leaving the prisoners for his support squad to pick up, he proceeded to mop up positions in the immediate area, capturing more prisoners and bringing his total count to 17.

Later that day, after he had reorganized his men and consolidated the newly captured ground, the enemy launched a fierce armored counterattack directly at his platoon positions. Securing a bazooka, Sgt. Barfoot took up an exposed position directly in front of 3 advancing Mark VI tanks. From a distance of 75 yards his first shot destroyed the track of the leading tank, effectively disabling it, while the other 2 changed direction toward the flank. As the crew of the disabled tank dismounted, Sgt. Barfoot killed 3 of them with his tommygun. He continued onward into enemy terrain and destroyed a recently abandoned German fieldpiece with a demolition charge placed in the breech. While returning to his platoon position, Sgt. Barfoot, though greatly fatigued by his Herculean efforts, assisted 2 of his seriously wounded men 1,700 yards to a position of safety.

Sgt. Barfoot's extraordinary heroism, demonstration of magnificent valor, and aggressive determination in the face of pointblank fire are a perpetual inspiration to his fellow soldiers.

A Medal Is Birthed in the Midst of War

On December 9, 1861 Iowa Senator James W. Grimes introduced a bill designed to "promote the efficiency of the Navy" by authorizing the production and distribution of "medals of honor." On December 21st the bill was passed, authorizing 200 such medals be produced "which shall be bestowed upon such petty officers, seamen, landsmen and marines as shall distinguish themselves by their gallantry in action and other seamanlike qualities during the present war (Civil War)." President Lincoln signed the bill and the Navy Medal of Honor was born.

Two months later, Massachusetts Senator Henry Wilson introduced a similar bill, this one to authorize "the President to distribute medals to privates in the Army of the United States who shall distinguish themselves in battle." Over the following months, wording changed slightly as the bill made its way through Congress. When President Abraham Lincoln signed it into law on July 14, 1862, the Army Medal of Honor was born. It read in part:

Resolved by the Senate and House of Representatives of the United States of America in Congress assembled, That the President of the United States be, and he is hereby, authorized to cause two thousand "medals of honor" to be prepared with suitable emblematic devices, and to direct that the same be presented, in the name of the Congress, to such non-commissioned officers and privates as shall most distinguish themselves by their gallantry in action, and other soldier-like qualities, during the present insurrection (Civil War).

With these two simple acts, Congress created a unique award that would achieve prominence in American history like few others.

Colonel Harvey C. Barnum, Jr.
U.S. Marine Corps (Ret.) • Vietnam

"At risk of oversimplification, I believe leaders (junior officers) will be effective: 1) if they are imbued with personal integrity, knowledge of their men and women, and concern for their welfare; 2) if they have technical and tactical competency resulting from training; 3) if they treat all subordinates with firmness, fairness, compassion, and dignity; and 4) if they demonstrate common sense, imagination, drive, and determination. Remember, good leadership is born of concern and nurtured by practice. I charge you to always be faithful to your God, your country, your family, and your Corps. *Semper Fidelis.*"

Rank and organization
Captain (then Lt.), U.S. Marine Corps, Company H,
2d Battalion, 9th Marines, 3d Marine Division (Rein).
Place and date
Ky Phu in Quang Tin Province, Republic of Vietnam, 12/18/65.

CITATION

For conspicuous gallantry and intrepidity at the risk of his life above and beyond the call of duty.

When the company was suddenly pinned down by a hail of extremely accurate enemy fire and was quickly separated from the remainder of the battalion by over 500 meters of open and fire-swept ground, and casualties mounted rapidly. Lt. Barnum quickly made a hazardous reconnaissance of the area, seeking targets for his artillery. Finding the rifle company commander mortally wounded and the radio operator killed, with complete disregard for his safety, he gave aid to the dying commander, then removed the radio from the dead operator and strapped it to himself. He immediately assumed command of the rifle company, and moving at once into the midst of the heavy fire, rallying and giving encouragement to all units, reorganized them to replace the loss of key personnel and led their attack on enemy positions from which deadly fire continued to come.

His sound and swift decisions and his obvious calm served to stabilize the badly decimated units and his gallant example as he stood exposed repeatedly to point out targets served as an inspiration to all. Provided with 2 armed helicopters, he moved fearlessly through enemy fire to control the air attack against the firmly entrenched enemy while skillfully directing 1 platoon in a successful counterattack on the key enemy positions. Having thus cleared a small area, he requested and directed the landing of 2 transport helicopters for the evacuation of the dead and wounded. He then assisted in the mopping up and final seizure of the battalion's objective.

His gallant initiative and heroic conduct reflected great credit upon himself and were in keeping with the highest traditions of the Marine Corps and the U.S. Naval Service.

Gary B. Beikirch
U.S. Army • Vietnam

"I would like to share with you two of the most significant experiences in my life. My experiences in Vietnam taught me many life-changing lessons: How precious life is...how frightening death is...and how important God is to both life and death. After being med-evaced from Vietnam, wounded three times, and spending almost a year in the hospital, I was left with questions that I could not answer, an anger I could not control, and a guilt that almost destroyed me. What I needed was my second experience.

"Two years after leaving Vietnam, a friend shared with me a simple but powerful message: God loved me.... He had forgiven me because His Son, Jesus Christ, died for me, and He wanted His Spirit to become the center of my life. God's allowing me to wear the Medal of Honor was only to open doors so I could share His love (Jer. 9:23-24; Ps. 49:20). Although this is not Scripture, the following quote had an immediate impact on me as soon as I read it. I first saw it in a Mike Force team house in Pleiku. 'To really live you must almost die. To those who fight for it...life has a meaning...the protected will never know!'"

Rank and organization
Sergeant, U.S. Army, Company B, 5th Special Forces Group,
1st Special Forces.
Place and date
Kontum Province, Republic of Vietnam, 4/1/70.

CITATION

For conspicuous gallantry and intrepidity in action at the risk of his life above and beyond the call of duty. Sgt. Beikirch, medical aidman, Detachment B-24, Company B, distinguished himself during the defense of Camp Dak Seang.

The allied defenders suffered a number of casualties as a result of an intense, devastating attack launched by the enemy from well-concealed positions surrounding the camp. Sgt. Beikirch, with complete disregard for his personal safety, moved unhesitatingly through the withering enemy fire to his fallen comrades, applied first aid to their wounds and assisted them to the medical aid station. When informed that a seriously injured American officer was lying in an exposed position, Sgt. Beikirch ran immediately through the hail of fire. Although he was wounded seriously by fragments from an exploding enemy mortar shell, Sgt. Beikirch carried the officer to a medical aid station. Ignoring his own serious injuries, Sgt. Beikirch left the relative safety of the medical bunker to search for and evacuate other men who had been injured. He was again wounded as he dragged a critically injured Vietnamese soldier to the medical bunker while simultaneously applying mouth-to-mouth resuscitation to sustain his life. Sgt. Beikirch again refused treatment and continued his search for other casualties until he collapsed. Only then did he permit himself to be treated. Sgt. Beikirch's complete devotion to the welfare of his comrades, at the risk of his life, are in keeping with the highest traditions of the military service and reflect great credit on him, his unit, and the U.S. Army.

FOR HIS HONOR

April 1st, 1970...over thirty years ago but I can still hear the screams, the explosions, the gunfire. April Fools day...if only it could have been a joke...but it was not. It was painfully real.

I was a member of a Green Beret Special Forces A team in Vietnam. Our peaceful Montagnard jungle camp was surrounded by 3 North Vietnamese regiments. Inside the camp of Dak Seang were 12 Americans and 2,300 Montagnard villagers, mostly women and children. It is still their screams and lifeless bodies that I remember even today.

Artillery and rockets began pounding the camp in the early morning and continued for hours. Then the "human wave" assault of ground troops began. Our jungle home had become a scene of horror, terror, and death.

Running across an open area, I saw a wounded Montagnard (we affectionately called them "Yards") lying on the ground. As I was trying to bandage his wounds, I heard "IT" coming, like a diesel train...more artillery...maybe a 122mm rocket. As I threw my body over the wounded man to shield him from the explosion, I felt like I had been kicked in the back by a horse. Shrapnel from the blasts had slammed into my back and abdomen. The concussion from the blast had thrown me about 25 feet into a wall of sandbags by our mortar pit. I tried to get up but could not move my legs. I remember thinking, "Well, at least I'm alive...and hey! There's a Purple Heart." I looked back to see what had happened to the "Yard" I was helping and all that was left was pieces...the explosion had torn him apart. How? Why? I was lying on top of him. Why was I still alive? These questions would plague me for years, but at that moment, there was too much to do.

Two other "Yards" came by and picked me up. They wanted to take me to the medical bunker but I yelled, "No!! We've got things to do up here." For hours they carried me as we treated the wounded, dragged bodies, distributed ammo, directed fire, and fought for our lives. As I continued to lose blood, I was getting weaker. Also by this time I was wounded two more times. I finally lost consciousness. When I awoke I realized they had taken me to the underground medical bunker. Pat, a new medic who had been in camp less than a week said, "Man, you're hurt bad. We got to get you out of here." I screamed out to my "Yards": "Get me out of here. If I am going to die, I am not going to die down here." A year of living with these "Yards" had developed a strong bond of love and trust between us. It was this bond that made them pick me up and carry me back out into the battle.

As the battle raged on, my two "Yard" friends carried me for hours, taking me where I directed them, helping me care for the wounded, shielding me, protecting me, holding me up as we continued to fight. Later, I would again be plagued by the questions of, "Why did they carry me all that time? Why did they stay with me?" They never left my side. What made their love for me so strong that they were willing to give their lives for me? One was killed as he saved my life.

At some point, I finally collapsed and was unable to go on. From here on my personal memories are a swirling stream of sporadic events...watching med-evac helicopters being shot down as they tried to get me out...strong arms reaching down and pulling me into the "warm belly" of a chopper, the face of the young medic shocked at seeing that I was still alive, but telling me I was going to be OK, being thrown onto a litter and rushed into an operating room, IVs in my arms and neck, catheters in every opening of my body, lights, shouting, and then...darkness.

I awoke not knowing how long I had been unconscious. I did a quick self exam...unable to move from my waist down (I would learn later that it was only a temporary injury, a shock to my spine and spinal cord from the shrapnel injury.) "What is that on my stomach?" My large intestine was in a plastic bag (shrapnel had perforated my large intestine and a colostomy had been done). More tubes were in my body...one through my nose and in the stomach...my stomach! Why did it hurt so? I looked down and realized it had been ripped open and was now sutured back together. Then darkness...I was once again unconscious. These periods of being "in and out of consciousness" continued...each time bringing new awareness. Once, I came to and watched as an Australian advisor fought for his last breath and lost. As they pulled the sheet over his head, I began drifting into unconsciousness and wondered if this was MY death.

I awoke once again but this time my waking moments were spent battling with the deaths of so many of my friends: the "Yard" I covered with my body, the one who carried me for hours...Why am I still alive and they are not? God, I feel so guilty, so helpless, so angry.

Days passed as I continued to come and go. One day I awoke and there was a chaplain standing by the next bed praying with a young dying soldier. He turned and saw my open eyes. "Glad to see you're awake. I've been praying for you for a couple of days. Would you like to pray?" My answer to his question was a pleading, "I don't know how." He simply replied, "That doesn't matter. God knows how to listen." My prayer was a simple one: "God I don't know if you're real. I don't know if you're here, but I'm scared and I need You."

Right then something happened...no flashes of light, no miraculous physical healing, no visions on the wall or by my bed, but a peace, a comfort, a "knowing" that there was Someone outside of myself who heard my prayer and wanted me to know that I was loved as I was never loved before.

The next two years were spent searching to find out more about this Presence, this God who had touched my life. I traveled around the country, through Canada, studied different philosophies, religions, searching for ways that might lead me once again to that Peace. My search led me to a small town on the ocean just south of Boston. I was visiting a friend and told him about Vietnam, the lessons it had taught me, the questions it had left with me, and my efforts to find God. He told me that there is no mystery to finding God. He then asked me to do him a favor and read a book. He handed me a New Testament.

As I read what Jesus taught about life, the heart of man, our need for forgiveness, and God's love for us, I knew that He was the One whom I had met in the hospital bed in Vietnam. He had seen my pain and my fear and had given me His Peace and Comfort. He also had been with me all those years as I was looking for more of that Peace. As I read more of His words I learned that He wanted me to know Him. He wanted to become a greater part of my life. He didn't want me to know about Him, He wanted me to KNOW HIM, to walk with Him, to love Him, and allow Him to love me.

After my discharge from the Army, I had planned on going to medical school. However, once I started walking with my new "Friend," I felt like He wanted me to do something different. I packed my bags, headed for Florida with a Bible, and stayed there for a couple of months praying and asking God what He wanted me to do. His answer to me was to go into the ministry.

In September of 1973, I entered seminary, dedicating my life to serving the God who had given me life. One night a few weeks later I received a phone call from Washington, D.C. asking me to come to Washington and be presented the Congressional Medal of Honor by President Nixon. Coincidence? I do not believe in coincidences any more...not when you are walking with God. However, among many other emotions I was also very confused. I knew I was not worthy of such an honor. God knew I wasn't worthy. But as I looked to Him for the reason, I believe He presented the honor to me so that it might "open doors" and allow others to hear about His desire to have a personal relationship with us through His Son, Jesus Christ.

God does have a plan and a purpose for our lives, and although there is no mystery to finding Him, at times it is a mystery to walk with Him. It wasn't easy for me at first. Even now there are times when I fail to trust His love completely, but then I remember my two "Yard" friends who loved me, protected me, and carried me when I couldn't walk. If I could trust them with my life, why shouldn't I be able to trust Jesus?

So each day I trust and walk humbly with Him...and I wear the Medal of Honor for Him and my two "Yard" friends.

—*Gary Beikirch*

Master Sergeant Roy P. Benavidez
U.S. Army (Ret.) • Vietnam

"Our youth need role models. They need to know and understand the price that has been paid for the freedom we enjoy. I always ask them to get an education, say no to drugs, and stay away from gangs. The youth of America will be our future leaders."

Rank and Organization
Master Sergeant, Detachment B-56,
5th Special Forces Group, Republic of Vietnam.
Place and Date
West of Loc Ninh on 2 May 1968.

CITATION
Master Sergeant (then Staff Sergeant) Roy P. Benavidez United States Army, who distinguished himself by a series of daring and extremely valorous actions on 2 May 1968 while assigned to Detachment B56, 5th Special Forces Group (Airborne), 1st Special Forces, Republic of Vietnam.

On the morning of 2 May 1968, a 12-man Special Forces Reconnaissance Team was inserted by helicopters in a dense jungle area west of Loc Ninh, Vietnam, to gather intelligence information about confirmed large-scale enemy activity. This area was controlled and routinely patrolled by the North Vietnamese Army. After a short period of time on the ground, the team met heavy enemy resistance, and requested emergency extraction. Three helicopters attempted extraction but were unable to land due to intense enemy small arms and anti-aircraft fire.

Sergeant Benavidez was at the Forward Operating Base in Loc Ninh monitoring the operation by radio when these helicopters returned to off-load wounded crewmembers and to assess aircraft damage. Sergeant Benavidez voluntarily boarded a returning aircraft to assist in another extraction attempt. Realizing that all the team members were either dead or wounded and unable to move to the pickup zone, he directed the aircraft to a nearby clearing where he jumped from the hovering helicopter and ran approximately 75 meters under withering small arms fire to the crippled team.

Prior to reaching the team's position he was wounded in his right leg, face, and head. Despite these painful injuries, he took charge, repositioning the team members and directing their fire to facilitate the landing of an extraction aircraft, and the loading of wounded and dead team members. He then threw smoke canisters to direct the aircraft to the team's position. Despite his severe wounds and under intense enemy fire, he carried and dragged half of the wounded team members to the awaiting aircraft. He then provided protective fire by running alongside the aircraft as it moved to pick up the remaining team members. As the enemy's fire intensified, he hurried to recover the body and classified documents on the dead team leader. When he reached the leader's body, Sergeant Benavidez was severely wounded by small arms fire in the abdomen and grenade fragments in his back. At nearly the same moment, the aircraft pilot was mortally wounded, and his helicopter crashed. Although in extremely critical condition due to his multiple wounds, Sergeant Benavidez secured the classified documents and made his way back to the wreckage, where he aided the wounded out of the overturned aircraft and gathered the stunned survivors into a defensive perimeter.

Under increasing enemy automatic weapons and grenade fire,

he moved around the perimeter distributing water and ammunition to his weary men, reinstilling in them a will to live and fight. Facing a buildup of enemy opposition with a beleaguered team, Sergeant Benavidez mustered his strength, began calling in tactical air strikes and directed the fire from supporting gunships to suppress the enemy's fire and so permit another extraction attempt. He was wounded again in his thigh by small arms fire while administering first aid to a wounded team member just before another extraction helicopter was able to land.

His indomitable spirit kept him going as he began to ferry his comrades to the craft. On his second trip with the wounded, he was clubbed from additional wounds to his head and arms before killing his adversary. He then continued under devastating fire to carry the wounded to the helicopter. Upon reaching the aircraft, he spotted and killed two enemy soldiers who were rushing the craft from an angle that prevented the aircraft door gunner from firing upon them. With little strength remaining, he made one last trip to the perimeter to ensure that all classified material had been collected or destroyed, and to bring in the remaining wounded. Only then, in extremely serious condition from numerous wounds and loss of blood, did he allow himself to be pulled into the extraction aircraft.

Sergeant Benavidez' gallant choice to join voluntarily his comrades who were in critical straits, to expose himself constantly to withering enemy fire, and his refusal to be stopped despite numerous severe wounds, saved the lives of at least eight men. His fearless personal leadership, tenacious devotion to duty, and extremely valorous actions in the face of overwhelming odds were in keeping with the highest traditions of the military service, and reflect the utmost credit on him and the United States Army.

The Symbolism of the Medal

The Navy's Medal of Honor was the first approved and the first designed. The initial work was done by the Philadelphia Mint at the request of Secretary of the Navy Gideon Welles.

The selected Medal of Honor design consisted of an inverted, 5-pointed star. On each of the five points was a cluster of laurel leaves to represent victory, mixed with a cluster of oak to represent strength.

Surrounding the encircled insignia were 34 stars, equal to the number of stars in the U.S. Flag at the time in 1862...one star for each state of the Union including the 11 Confederate states. The stars are also symbolic of the "heavens and the divine goal which man has aspired to since time immemorial" according to Charles Thompson, Secretary of the Continental Congress back in 1777.

Inside the circle of 34 stars were engraved two images. To the right is the image of Minerva, the Roman symbol of wisdom and war. On her helmet is perched an owl, representing wisdom. In keeping with the Roman tradition, her left hand holds a bundle of rods and an ax blade, symbolic of authority. The shield in her right hand is the shield of the Union of our states (similar to the shield on our seal and other important emblems).

Recoiling from Minerva is a man clutching snakes in his hands, who represented discord. Taken in the context of the Civil War soldiers and sailors struggling to overcome the discord of the states and preserve the Union, the design was as fitting as it was symbolic.

Melvin E. Biddle
U.S. Army • WWII

"We are so lucky to live in the United States. My advice for life is: Always be honest and do what is right."

Rank and organization
Private First Class, U.S. Army, Company B,
517th Parachute Infantry Regiment.
Place and date
Near Soy, Belgium, 23-24 December 1944.

CITATION

He displayed conspicuous gallantry and intrepidity in action against the enemy near Soy, Belgium, on 23 and 24 December 1944.

Serving as lead scout during an attack to relieve the enemy-encircled town of Hotton, he aggressively penetrated a densely wooded area, advanced 400 yards until he came within range of intense enemy rifle fire, and within 20 yards of enemy positions, killed 3 snipers with unerring marksmanship. Courageously continuing his advance an additional 200 yards, he discovered a hostile machinegun position and dispatched its 2 occupants. He then located the approximate position of a well-concealed enemy machinegun nest, and crawling forward threw hand grenades which killed two Germans and fatally wounded a third. After signaling his company to advance, he entered a determined line of enemy defense, coolly and deliberately shifted his position, and shot 3 more enemy soldiers. Undaunted by enemy fire, he crawled within 20 yards of a machinegun nest, tossed his last hand grenade into the position, and after the explosion, charged the emplacement firing his rifle. When night fell, he scouted enemy positions alone for several hours and returned with valuable information which enabled our attacking infantry and armor to knock out 2 enemy tanks.

At daybreak he again led the advance and, when flanking elements were pinned down by enemy fire, without hesitation made his way toward a hostile machinegun position and from a distance of 50 yards killed the crew and 2 supporting riflemen. The remainder of the enemy, finding themselves without automatic weapon support, fled panic stricken.

Pfc. Biddle's intrepid courage and superb daring during his 20-hour action enabled his battalion to break the enemy grasp on Hotton with a minimum of casualties.

Major General Patrick Brady
U.S. Army (Ret.) • Vietnam

"I believe you will agree with me that there is one virtue that is key to all others for it secures them—courage. No other virtue, not freedom, not justice, not anything, not anyone, is safe without courage. Courage then, both physical and moral, is also the first trait of leadership.

"I believe the key to courage is faith. In combat, I coped with fear through my faith. It's a great source of calm, of comfort, and it gave me great confidence. I think because of my faith I was able to do things that, for me, would have otherwise been impossible."

Rank and organization
Major, U.S. Army, Medical Service Corps, 54th Medical Detachment, 67th Medical Group, 44th Medical Brigade.
Place and date
Near Chu Lai, Republic of Vietnam, 1/6/68.

CITATION
For conspicuous gallantry and intrepidity in action at the risk of

his life above and beyond the call of duty, Maj. Brady distinguished himself while serving in the Republic of Vietnam commanding a UH-1H ambulance helicopter, volunteered to rescue wounded men from a site in enemy held territory which was reported to be heavily defended and to be blanketed by fog.

To reach the site he descended through heavy fog and smoke and hovered slowly along a valley trail, turning his ship sideward to blow away the fog with the backwash from his rotor blades. Despite the unchallenged, close-range enemy fire, he found the dangerously small site, where he successfully landed and evacuated 2 badly wounded South Vietnamese soldiers.

He was then called to another area completely covered by dense fog where American casualties lay only 50 meters from the enemy. Two aircraft had previously been shot down and others had made unsuccessful attempts to reach this site earlier in the day. With unmatched skill and extraordinary courage, Maj. Brady made 4 flights to this embattled landing zone and successfully rescued all the wounded.

On his third mission of the day Maj. Brady once again landed at a site surrounded by the enemy. The friendly ground force, pinned down by enemy fire, had been unable to reach and secure the landing zone. Although his aircraft had been badly damaged and his controls partially shot away during his initial entry into this area, he returned minutes later and rescued the remaining injured.

Shortly thereafter, obtaining a replacement aircraft, Maj. Brady was requested to land in an enemy minefield where a platoon of American soldiers was trapped. A mine detonated near his helicopter, wounding 2 crewmembers and damaging his ship. In spite of this, he managed to fly 6 severely injured patients to medical aid.

Throughout that day Maj. Brady utilized 3 helicopters to evacuate a total of 51 seriously wounded men, many of whom would have perished without prompt medical treatment. Maj. Brady's bravery was in the highest traditions of the military service and reflects great credit upon himself and the U.S. Army.

GOD'S LIGHT IN THE
DARKNESS AND DOUBT

In my youth, I attended 10 different schools the first 9 years of my schooling. My brothers and I were herded from relative to relative and in and out of boarding schools. We were in Catholic schools on and off and boarded with Christian Brothers of Ireland where I developed and found great comfort in my faith. Without parents or lasting friendships, the Brothers and Nuns became my mentors. I learned early on that the only lasting relationship one has is with our self and with God. Some long forgotten Brother or Nun convinced me that I always had a friend in Jesus, and just talk to Him.

I enjoyed the quiet time at Mass and Jesus became my one true friend and mentor. I got in the habit of talking through my problems with Him, not always in a prayerful way but casually in the heat of competition or what was at the time a desperate need. I do to this day. Success for me in any endeavor was based on my state of grace and my state of friendship with the Lord. If I was doing well in these areas, I knew He would listen to me.

I was a Dustoff pilot in Vietnam. Our job was to pick up the wounded from the battlefield much like 9-1-1 ambulances do from the streets of America. One in three of the Dustoff crews became a casualty in this work. More of those casualties were the result of a combination of night and weather than enemy action. Dustoff was the most effective combat operating system in that war. Survival rates of our combat troops were phenomenal and, in fact, there was a greater chance of survival if you were shot in the jungles of Vietnam than if you were in an accident on the highways of America.

During my first tour in Vietnam, most of my flying was done in the Delta, a large force landing area. There was not a lot of relief. It was mostly flat, moist terrain with few mountains. In addition, it was filled with canals connecting every possible pick-up site. Even in the roughest weather, and at night, one need only get on a canal and follow it through intersections to the patients. You could turn on your landing light, or searchlight, or both, and hover along at low-level much like driving from point to point on a highway. Day or night, it was difficult to keep us from a patient.

You can imagine my concern when I returned for a second tour, this time to the mountains of I Corps. We were in Chu Lai, just south of Danang. The terrain along the coast was flat and full of rice paddies, much like the Delta, but unfortunately it gave way inland to rugged mountainous terrain. This was where most of the fighting took place. It was an area of violent storms characterized by thick early morning fog that covered the valleys about 500 feet up the mountains. In the afternoons you could expect the tops of the mountains, key military terrain, to be covered with clouds about 500 feet down. This was the type of weather and terrain that killed so many of my fellow Dustoff crewmembers.

My concern was heightened by the fact that all but two of the pilots in the unit were right out of flight school with no experience in combat. There was nothing in flight school to match the challenges they would face in this terrain and the intensity of combat that existed upon our arrival. In fact, all six of our aircraft were damaged by enemy fire on one day in the first week we were operational. Of the 40 men in this detachment, 23 would get Purple Heart medals within 10 months. But it wasn't the enemy that concerned me as we moved the unit from Fort Benning and began to set up operations at Chu Lai. There was no way to avoid him. It was the weather and the mountains that terrified me.

For those who have heard the anguish of a soldier pleading for someone to come and save the life of his buddy, there is nothing else in life to equal it. The challenge was always to save that life and not kill the 4 crew members on your chopper doing it. To do this you had to overcome the challenges of nearby enemy fire, the terrain, and the limitations of the aircraft and those operating it. And all of this had to be done in a timely manner. The troops could die if you waited for the fire or weather to lift, or for the sun to rise.

As I mentioned, the first week was murderous; several crew members were hurt and all our aircraft damaged. But no one was killed, and we had not come face to face with night weather missions or tropical storms.

It had to happen. We got a call one evening about a soldier who was bitten by a snake at a fire support base on one of the mountains just west of Chu Lai. As I approached the area I saw to my horror that the mountain-top was engulfed in thick clouds. As always, I turned to God for help. What in the heck did He want me to do? To fly into zero-zero weather without being on an approved flight plan on instruments to a proper let-down facility was against all flight regulations. A mishap under those conditions could end my career even if no one was hurt. I was required to turn back. By this time the troops were on the radio screaming that the patient had gone into convulsions. They were begging for help. God gave me a hint. I knew I had to try. I started head-first up the mountain right above the trees.

The good news was that if I got disoriented, I could fall away from the mountain and I would break out in the valley. And that is what happened several times. The troops were pleading for me to help them and I was pleading with God to help me. The crew was very tense. (I had on board a new mechanic and this was his first mission. He refused to fly again after this mission.) Each time I got in the clouds I would get disoriented and, with much luck, be able to fall into the valley. On what I promised to be the last try, I really messed up. We were blown sideways and I was looking out my side window for a place to go in when I discovered that I could see the tip of my rotor blade and the tops of the trees. I had two reference points, and I knew I was right side up. Thank you, my good Lord. I turned that baby sideways and hovered up the mountain watching the blade and the treetops, right into the area. The troops were delighted and we got the patient to the hospital. As a bonus on this mission someone said "God bless you, Double Nickel" (my call sign) on the radio. I knew God had blessed us although I was a little upset that He took what I thought was a bit too long to do it.

I did not get court-martialed and, in fact, used this technique many times for several of the missions on the day I was to receive the Medal of Honor. In the citation they said I flew sideways and blew away the fog. That was the only way they could explain it since one cannot fly visually in instrument conditions. God taught me that such is not the case. The truth is that you can see about 40 feet in the thickest stuff and if you have a second reference point, you can go anywhere, albeit slowly. Some day when you are on an airplane in the clouds look out the wing or when you are driving in the rain, compare your visibility out an open side window with the visibility out the windshield, and you will see what I mean.

We had solved the low valley fog and the mountain top cloud problem, but the night weather mission was still lurking. The call came during the night in the middle of a tropical storm. I was already sweating before we had all the information. The unit had suffered several loads of casualties in the valley beyond the mountains. Okay, Lord, what now? I started with the technique we used in the Delta and tried to stay under the weather and hover forward. I turned my searchlight on and had the crew lie on the floor and look out the door to the rear. The lights of a village were kept in sight as we hovered from light to light into the mountains.

It was pouring rain and the searchlight reflected off the rain and blinded me. It was like flying in an inkwell in front and we were losing the lights to the rear. I knew I would hit a mountain if we went any further, and it would eventually require instruments to fly. I had a bird that was not fully instrumented and that was risky. I decided to go north to a break in the mountains and see if I could follow a river down into the patient area as I had done with canals in the Delta. I was in my usual mode of conversation with God, wondering why He was doing this to me, and how He was going to help me get those patients out. I got to the river and had the same problem with the blinding rain and the searchlight. Then I had a vision. Thank you, dear Jesus.

On a previous night mission I had flown a routine pickup into the valley that we called "Death Valley." As I sat on the ground loading the patients, I was enjoying the usual paradoxical beauty of the night on the battlefield. The flares drifted down through the mountains illuminating the beautiful landscape in light and dark multiple shades of green pierced occasionally with the deadly but beautiful mesmerizing streaks of tracer fire. I absentmindedly looked up and noticed that one of the mountains was covered with clouds but in perfect silhouette from the flares.

The vision came back to me and I now knew how to get those guys out. I called back to the base and told them to get me a bird with good instrumentation. My plan was to fly instruments above the mountains to the pickup site and then let down into the mountain visually using flares. We would use our FM homing device to find the patients. Once we had the patients on board, I would do a steep instrument take off into the clouds and weather above the mountains, fly out over the coast and let down over the water near the lights of Chu Lai. That's what I did, four times. I used 3 copilots that night but got all the patients out.

We used this technique on other occasions and never failed to get the patients. We now had solutions to the night weather problem. As I said, we had 23 Purple Heart medals, but we never lost an aircraft or a crew member due to the night or the weather. This was despite the fact that we flew thousands of night and weather missions, had some 117% of our aircraft damaged by enemy fire each month and carried over 20,000 patients in 10 months. In the three months following our tour, the same small unit had 5 crew members killed. God had certainly watched over us.

I received the Distinguished Service Cross for the night flare mission and numerous other awards for my flying in Vietnam. As a result, one encyclopedia lists me as the war's top helicopter pilot. The truth is that I was an average pilot who came within an eyelash of busting out of flight school. My instructor pilot said I was dangerous and there are to this day some of my copilots who will swear I can't read a map. There is no way I could have flown the missions I flew on my own. I will not say that God was my copilot because I could not have made it without the copilots I had. For my part, I had a strong faith that shielded me from fear, and I cared about the troops. But it was God who showed me the way, who was my Light as I stumbled through the darkness and the fog and the clouds of my doubts.

—Pat Brady

Over the Years...

Since its original inception, much of the symbolism in the Medal of Honor has not changed. The Army MOH was created soon after the original Navy MOH in 1862. It included an eagle, symbolizing the United States of America, perched on a cannon with a saber grasped in its talons.

In 1904 the Gillespie version of the MOH included a simple portrait of a helmeted Minerva to replace the "Minerva repelling discord" scene. The red, white and blue ribbon was replaced with light blue and 13 white stars, once again representing the original 13 colonies.

In 1919 the Tiffany Cross version of the MOH had a Maltese Cross instead of an inverted star. The Maltese Cross' eight points symbolize the 8 virtues of a knight. A cross itself also represents the four cardinal directions and the sun. This design was discontinued in 1942 due to its unpopularity.

In 1965 the Air Force MOH was created and it replaced the Minerva portrait with the head of the Statue of Liberty. Lady Liberty has a pointed crown instead of a helmet.

Paul W. Bucha
U.S. Army • Vietnam

"If there is one trait that is apparent when one witnesses a gathering of Medal of Honor recipients, it is that, as a group, they appear to be just like any group of randomly selected men. Some are tall; some are short. Some are young; some are older. They are all races and ethnicities. In short, they are like you and me. But within each of them was the potential, when that mysterious confluence of time and events occurred, to resist the destiny apparent at the time and to change fate and change history.

"The lesson learned is that each of us, each everyday person, has within them the potential should they be called upon or should they choose to do so, to challenge fate and change the destiny before them. We should recognize that potential and celebrate it each day of our lives. If one day we learn to treat each other with the respect this wonderful potential deserves, and without the need for a Medal of Honor, then this society will have made the most magnificent contribution to history possible."

Rank and organization
Captain, U.S. Army, Company D, 3d Battalion,
187th Infantry, 3d Brigade, 101st Airborne Division.
Place and date
Near Phuoc Vinh, Binh Duong Province,
Republic of Vietnam, 16- 19 March 1968.

CITATION

For conspicuous gallantry and intrepidity in action at the risk of his life above and beyond the call of duty. Capt. Bucha distinguished himself while serving as commanding officer, Company D, on a reconnaissance-in-force mission against enemy forces near Phuoc Vinh.

The company was inserted by helicopter into the suspected enemy stronghold to locate and destroy the enemy. During this period, Capt. Bucha aggressively and courageously led his men in the destruction of enemy fortifications and base areas and eliminated scattered resistance impeding the advance of the company. On 18 March while advancing to contact, the lead elements of the company became engaged by the heavy automatic weapon, heavy machine gun, rocket-propelled grenade, Claymore mine and small-arms fire of an estimated battalion-size force. Capt. Bucha, with complete disregard for his safety, moved to the threatened area to direct the defense and ordered reinforcements to the aid of the lead element. Seeing that his men were pinned down by heavy machine gun fire from a concealed bunker located some 40 meters to the front of the positions, Capt. Bucha crawled through the hail of fire to single-handedly destroy the bunker with grenades.

During this heroic action, Capt. Bucha received a painful shrapnel wound. Returning to the perimeter, he observed that his unit could not hold its positions and repel the human wave assaults launched by the determined enemy. Capt. Bucha ordered the withdrawal of the unit elements and covered the withdrawal to positions of a company perimeter from which he could direct fire upon the charging enemy. When 1 friendly element retrieving casualties was ambushed and cut off from the perimeter, Capt. Bucha ordered them to feign death and he directed artillery fire around them.

During the night, Capt. Bucha moved throughout the position, distributing ammunition, providing encouragement and insuring the integrity of the defense. He directed artillery, helicopter gunship and Air Force gunship fire on the enemy strong points and attacking forces, marking the positions with smoke grenades. Using flashlights in complete view of enemy snipers, he directed the medical evacuation of 3 air-ambulance loads of seriously wounded personnel and the helicopter supply of his company. At daybreak Capt. Bucha led a rescue party to recover the dead and wounded members of the ambushed element. During the period of intensive combat, Capt. Bucha, by his extraordinary heroism, inspirational example, outstanding leadership, and professional competence, led his company in the decimation of a superior enemy force, which left 156 dead on the battlefield.

His bravery and gallantry at the risk of his life are in the highest traditions of the military service, Capt. Bucha has reflected great credit on himself, his unit, and the U.S. Army.

Medal and Ribbons

The ribbon that held the medal was originally a blue bar on top and 13 red and white stripes running vertically. The 13 represents the original 13 colonies. The color white represents purity and innocence; red represents hardiness, valor, and blood; blue signifies vigilance, perseverance, and justice. The stripes also represent the rays of the sun.

On May 2, 1895 Congress authorized "a rosette or knot to be worn in lieu of the medal and a ribbon to be worn with the medal." Today's Medal of Honor Ribbon is blue with FIVE stars, 2 at the top and 3 at the bottom. (One of the most common mistakes people make when displaying Medal of Honor graphics is to display the ribbon up-side down.)

The six-sided blue silk rosette bears 13 stars and is worn on civilian attire. Medal of Honor recipients also wear the Medal itself around the neck of civilian attire for special occasions.

Though it was not uncommon for Medals of Honor to continue to be pinned to a soldier's tunic during World War II, the practice of draping it around a recipient's neck became increasingly used. For this purpose the modern Medal of Honor was suspended from an 8-sided "pad" bearing 13 white stars, to which the blue silk neck ribbon was attached.

The Medal of Honor is the only United States Military Award that is worn around the neck rather than pinned to the uniform.

Captain James M. Burt
U.S. Army (Ret.) • WWII

"Be prepared, be positive, be honest! If it has to be done, do it! Don't look back morosely; think back if appropriate...intelligently. Seek and accept all cross training possible. If the job is messy—then do it yourself instead of ordering someone else to do it. Trust horizontally, trust vertically, have faith."

Rank and organization
Captain, U.S. Army, Company B, 66th Armored Regiment, 2d Armored Division.
Place and date
Near Wurselen, Germany, 10/13/44.

CITATION
Capt. James M. Burt was in command of Company B, 66th Armored Regiment on the western outskirts of Wurselen, Germany, on 13 October 1944, when his organization participated in a coordinated infantry-tank attack destined to isolate the large German garrison which was tenaciously defending the city of Aachen.

In the first day's action, when infantrymen ran into murderous small-arms and mortar fire, Capt. Burt dismounted from his tank about 200 yards to the rear and moved forward on foot beyond the infantry positions, where, as the enemy concentrated a tremendous volume of fire upon him, he calmly motioned his tanks into good firing positions. As the attack gained momentum, he climbed aboard his tank and directed the action from the rear deck, exposed to hostile volleys which finally wounded him painfully in the face and neck. He maintained his dangerous post despite pointblank self-propelled gunfire until friendly artillery knocked out these enemy weapons, and then proceeded to the advanced infantry scouts' positions to deploy his tanks for the defense of the gains which had been made.

The next day, when the enemy counterattacked, he left cover and went 75 yards through heavy fire to assist the infantry battalion commander who was seriously wounded. For the next 8 days, through rainy, miserable weather and under constant, heavy shelling, Capt. Burt held the combined forces together, dominating and controlling the critical situation through the sheer force of his heroic example. To direct artillery fire, on 15 October, he took his tank 300 yards into the enemy lines, where he dismounted and remained for 1 hour giving accurate data to friendly gunners.

Twice more that day he went into enemy territory under deadly fire on reconnaissance. In succeeding days he never faltered in his determination to defeat the strong German forces opposing him. Twice the tank in which he was riding was knocked out by enemy action, and each time he climbed aboard another vehicle and continued the fight. He took great risks to rescue wounded comrades and inflicted prodigious destruction on enemy personnel and materiel even though suffering from the wounds he received in the battle's opening phase.

Capt. Burt's intrepidity and disregard of personal safety were so complete that his own men and the infantry who attached themselves to him were inspired to overcome the wretched and extremely hazardous conditions which accompanied one of the most bitter local actions of the war. The victory achieved closed the Aachen gap.

Robert E. Bush
U.S. Navy • WWII

"My life started with a single parent, my sister, and me in the 1920s. We lived in a hospital my mother ran as Matron R.N. After one boarding school after another, I recognized the want and need for a sound family environment.

"I married Wanda at 18 and we started down the road of life. Fifty-two years later with a proud family of four children we reflect on how we got here. A good life begins with a good job.

"Our basic rule of life is to do unto others as we would have them do unto us. Honesty is the best policy. The most important four-letter word in our house is work. Religion is an important part of our life; however, God helps those who help themselves. With these simple rules we have managed to raise and educate four children. We have nine grandchildren and six great-grandchildren.

"With the help of God and a few Marines, we are happy, contented, and count our blessings every day."

Rank and organization
Hospital Apprentice First Class, U.S. Naval Reserve, serving as
Medical Corpsman with a rifle company, 2d Battalion,
5th Marines, 1st Marine Division.
Place and date
Okinawa Jima, Ryukyu Islands, 2 May 1945.

CITATION

For conspicuous gallantry and intrepidity at the risk of his life above and beyond the call of duty while serving as Medical Corpsman with a rifle company, in action against enemy Japanese forces on Okinawa Jima, Ryukyu Islands, 2 May 1945.

Fearlessly braving the fury of artillery, mortar, and machinegun fire from strongly entrenched hostile positions, Bush constantly and unhesitatingly moved from one casualty to another to attend the wounded falling under the enemy's murderous barrages. As the attack passed over a ridge top, Bush was advancing to administer blood plasma to a marine officer lying wounded on the skyline when the Japanese launched a savage counterattack. In this perilously exposed position, he resolutely maintained the flow of life-giving plasma. With the bottle held high in one hand, Bush drew his pistol with the other and fired into the enemy's ranks until his ammunition was expended. Quickly seizing a discarded carbine, he trained his fire on the Japanese charging pointblank over the hill, accounting for 6 of the enemy despite his own serious wounds and the loss of one eye suffered during his desperate battle in defense of the helpless man.

With the hostile force finally routed, he calmly disregarded his own critical condition to complete his mission, valiantly refusing medical treatment for himself until his officer patient had been evacuated, and collapsing only after attempting to walk to the battle aid station.

His daring initiative, great personal valor, and heroic spirit of self-sacrifice in service of others reflect great credit upon Bush and enhance the finest traditions of the U.S. Naval Service.

Hector A. Cafferata, Jr.
U.S. Marine Corps • Korea

"In combat, my greatest fear was not dying or being wounded. My greatest concern was to never let my friends, other Marines, down. My advice is: Always do the best you can do. If you do your best, you will be able to live with yourself.

"A number of years after the Korean War, I spoke with one of the Marines in my unit. He was miserable because he believed that he had not done all he could have done during the war. I tried to reassure him that we all did what we could.

"If you always try to do what you know is right and do the best that you can, you will be able to look at yourself in the mirror each morning and accept what you see. Do your best. That is all anyone can ask."

Rank and organization
Private, U.S. Marine Corps Reserve, Company F, 2d Battalion, 7th Marines, 1st Marine Division (Rein.).
Place and date
Korea, 28 November 1950.

CITATION

For conspicuous gallantry and intrepidity at the risk of his life above and beyond the call of duty while serving as a rifleman with Company F, in action against enemy aggressor forces.

When all the other members of his fire team became casualties, creating a gap in the lines, during the initial phase of a vicious attack launched by a fanatical enemy of regimental strength against his company's hill position, Pvt. Cafferata waged a lone battle with grenades and rifle fire as the attack gained momentum and the enemy threatened penetration through the gap and endangered the integrity of the entire defensive perimeter. Making a target of himself under the devastating fire from automatic weapons, rifles, grenades, and mortars, he maneuvered up and down the line and delivered accurate and effective fire against the onrushing force, killing 15, wounding many more, and forcing the others to withdraw so that reinforcements could move up and consolidate the position.

Again fighting desperately against a renewed onslaught later that same morning when a hostile grenade landed in a shallow entrenchment occupied by wounded marines, Pvt. Cafferata rushed into the gully under heavy fire, seized the deadly missile in his right hand and hurled it free of his comrades before it detonated, severing part of 1 finger and seriously wounding him in the right hand and arm. Courageously ignoring the intense pain, he staunchly fought on until he was struck by a sniper's bullet and forced to submit to evacuation for medical treatment.

Stouthearted and indomitable, Pvt. Cafferata, by his fortitude, great personal valor, and dauntless perseverance in the face of almost certain death, saved the lives of several of his fellow marines and contributed essentially to the success achieved by his company in maintaining its defensive position against tremendous odds. His extraordinary heroism throughout was in keeping with the highest traditions of the U.S. Naval Service.

Sergeant Major Jon R. Cavaiani
U.S. Army (Ret.) • Vietnam

"If I were to offer my advice about a creed or code of conduct for life and about success and significance, I would offer the advice given to me by my father. When I asked him how he became a success, he told me, 'Honesty and making the right decision were the major factors that helped me through life.' He also said that before he made a decision to do something, he asked himself three simple questions: 'Will what I do hurt my family? Will it hurt my friends? And lastly, will it hurt myself? If I can answer yes to any of these questions, I don't do it.' He believed your word is your bond. I have lived by these words throughout my life."

Rank and organization
Staff Sergeant, U.S. Army, Vietnam Training
Advisory Group, Republic of Vietnam.
Place and date
Republic of Vietnam, 4 and 5 June 1971.

CITATION

S/Sgt. Cavaiani distinguished himself by conspicuous gallantry and intrepidity at the risk of life above and beyond the call of duty in action in the Republic of Vietnam on 4 and 5 June 1971 while serving as a platoon leader to a security platoon, providing security for an isolated radio relay site located within enemy-held territory.

On the morning of 4 June 1971, the entire camp came under an intense barrage of enemy small arms, automatic weapons, rocket-propelled grenade and mortar fire from a superior size enemy force. S/Sgt. Cavaiani acted with complete disregard for his personal safety as he repeatedly exposed himself to heavy enemy fire in order to move about the camp's perimeter directing the platoon's fire and rallying the platoon in a desperate fight for survival. S/Sgt. Cavaiani also returned heavy suppressive fire upon the assaulting enemy force during this period with a variety of weapons.

When the entire platoon was to be evacuated, S/Sgt. Cavaiani unhesitatingly volunteered to remain on the ground and direct the helicopters into the landing zone. S/Sgt. Cavaiani was able to direct the first 3 helicopters in evacuating a major portion of the platoon. Due to intense increase in enemy fire, S/Sgt. Cavaiani was forced to remain at the camp overnight where he calmly directed the remaining platoon members in strengthening their defenses.

On the morning of 5 June, a heavy ground fog restricted visibility. The superior size enemy force launched a major ground attack in an attempt to completely annihilate the remaining small force. The enemy force advanced in 2 ranks, first firing a heavy volume of small arms automatic weapons and rocket-propelled grenade fire while the second rank continuously threw a steady barrage of hand grenades at the beleaguered force. S/Sgt. Cavaiani returned a heavy barrage of small arms and hand grenade fire on the assaulting enemy force but was unable to slow them down. He ordered the remaining platoon members to attempt to escape while he provided them with cover fire. With one last courageous exertion, S/Sgt. Cavaiani recovered a machine gun, stood up, completely exposing himself to the heavy enemy fire directed at him, and began firing the machine gun in a sweeping motion along the 2 ranks of advancing enemy soldiers. Through S/Sgt. Cavaiani's valiant efforts with complete disregard for his safety, the majority of the remaining platoon members were able to escape. While inflicting severe losses on the advancing enemy force, S/Sgt. Cavaiani was wounded numerous times.

S/Sgt. Cavaiani's conspicuous gallantry, extraordinary heroism and intrepidity at the risk of his life, above and beyond the call of duty, were in keeping with the highest traditions of the military service and reflect great credit upon himself and the U.S. Army.

Distribution of MOH Awards

2405 Army Medals
- 2338 awards to 2334 Soldiers
  (4 Soldiers were double recipients)
- 4 awards to Army Air Service (WWI)
- 38 awards to Army Air Corps (WWII)
- 4 awards to Air Force (Korean War)
- 6 awards to civilians
- 6 awards to Marines
  (5 of these were double awards)
- 9 Awards to Unknown Soldiers

1041 Navy Medals
- 743 awards to 735 Sailors
  (8 Sailors were Double Recipients)
- 295 awards to 293 Marines*
  (2 Marines were double recipients)
  (5 Marines also received Army MOH)
- Coast Guard Awardee
- 2 awards to civilians

*One WWI Marine received ONLY the Army award bringing the total number of awards to Marines to 296.

13 Air Force Medals
- all awarded for Vietnam service

BY STATE
Medals of Honor have been accredited to men in every state except Alaska. One Alaska resident did receive the Medal of Honor but entered service in Washington State, to which his award is accredited. Also, during World War II, one soldier received the Medal for heroism on the battlefields of Alaska. Thus every state does have a unique association to the Medal.

HMCM William R. Charette
U.S. Navy (Ret.) • Korea

"I don't feel like I have much to contribute, but if asked for advice about a creed or code of conduct I would say, 'Do unto others as you would have them do unto you.' I have always tried to live by the Golden Rule.

"My parents died when I was five years old, and I was raised by my aunt and uncle. They were good, God-fearing people. They raised me with this advice, and they demonstrated the Golden Rule by their example."

Rank and organization
Hospital Corpsman Third Class, U.S. Navy Medical Corpsman serving with a marine rifle company.
Place and date
Korea, 3/27/53.

CITATION
For conspicuous gallantry and intrepidity at the risk of his life above and beyond the call of duty in action against enemy aggressor forces during the early morning hours.

Participating in a fierce encounter with a cleverly concealed and well-entrenched enemy force occupying positions on a vital and bitterly contested outpost far in advance of the main line of resistance, HC3c. Charette repeatedly and unhesitatingly moved about through a murderous barrage of hostile small-arms and mortar fire to render assistance to his wounded comrades. When an enemy grenade landed within a few feet of a marine he was attending, he immediately threw himself upon the stricken man and absorbed the entire concussion of the deadly missile with his body. Although sustaining painful facial wounds, and undergoing shock from the intensity of the blast which ripped the helmet and medical aid kit from his person, HC3c. Charette resourcefully improvised emergency bandages by tearing off part of his clothing, and gallantly continued to administer medical aid to the wounded in his own unit and to those in adjacent platoon areas as well.

Observing a seriously wounded comrade whose armored vest had been torn from his body by the blast from an exploding shell, he selflessly removed his own battle vest and placed it upon the helpless man although fully aware of the added jeopardy to himself. Moving to the side of another casualty who was suffering excruciating pain from a serious leg wound, HC3c. Charette stood upright in the trench line and exposed himself to a deadly hail of enemy fire in order to lend more effective aid to the victim and to alleviate his anguish while being removed to a position of safety.

By his indomitable courage and inspiring efforts in behalf of his wounded comrades, HC3c. Charette was directly responsible for saving many lives. His great personal valor reflects the highest credit upon himself and enhances the finest traditions of the U.S. Naval Service.

Lieutenant Colonel Ernest Childers
U.S. Army (Ret.) • WWII

"For every element of freedom we have in this great country, we must use an equal amount of responsibility. I strive to encourage young people to become good, law-abiding, and patriotic citizens of this beautiful land. When young citizens ask me about my views on war, I explain how war—real war—is nothing as portrayed in the movies. I explain that the ugly side of war requires soldiers and citizens to defend our country, and ultimately, at times, it is necessary to take a life in order to preserve your own life or your fellow soldiers' lives."

Rank and organization
Second Lieutenant, U.S. Army, 45th Infantry Division.
Place and date
At Oliveto, Italy, 22 September 1943.

CITATION

For conspicuous gallantry and intrepidity at risk of life above and beyond the call of duty in action on 22 September 1943, at Oliveto, Italy.

Although 2d Lt. Childers previously had just suffered a fractured instep he, with 8 enlisted men, advanced up a hill toward enemy machinegun nests. The group advanced to a rock wall overlooking a cornfield and 2d Lt. Childers ordered a base of fire laid across the field so that he could advance.

When he was fired upon by two enemy snipers from a nearby house, he killed both of them. He moved behind the machinegun nests and killed all occupants of the nearer one. He continued toward the second one and threw rocks into it. When the two occupants of the nest raised up, he shot one. The other was killed by one of the eight enlisted men. 2d Lt. Childers continued his advance toward a house farther up the hill, and single-handedly captured an enemy mortar observer.

The exceptional leadership, initiative, calmness under fire, and conspicuous gallantry displayed by 2d Lt. Childers were an inspiration to his men.

Mike Colalillo
U.S. Army • WWII

"To have fought and died for my country would have been the ultimate sacrifice, but to have fought and lived has a greater reward—that of enjoying the freedom that is available to all of us. The good Lord allowed me to return home and I am forever grateful."

Rank and organization
Private First Class, U.S. Army, Company C,
398th Infantry, 100th Infantry Division.
Place and date
Near Untergriesheim, Germany, 7 April 1945.

CITATION

He was pinned down with other members of his company during an attack against strong enemy positions in the vicinity of Untergriesheim, Germany.

Heavy artillery, mortar, and machinegun fire made any move hazardous when he stood up, shouted to the company to follow, and ran forward in the wake of a supporting tank, firing his machine pistol. Inspired by his example, his comrades advanced in the face of savage enemy fire. When his weapon was struck by shrapnel and rendered useless, he climbed to the deck of a friendly tank, manned an exposed machinegun on the turret of the vehicle, and, while bullets rattled about him, fired at an enemy emplacement with such devastating accuracy that he killed or wounded at least 10 hostile soldiers and destroyed their machinegun. Maintaining his extremely dangerous post as the tank forged ahead, he blasted 3 more positions, destroyed another machinegun emplacement and silenced all resistance in his area, killing at least 3 and wounding an undetermined number of riflemen as they fled. His machinegun eventually jammed, so he secured a submachinegun from the tank crew to continue his attack on foot. When our armored forces exhausted their ammunition and the order to withdraw was given, he remained behind to help a seriously wounded comrade over several hundred yards of open terrain rocked by an intense enemy artillery and mortar barrage.

By his intrepidity and inspiring courage Pfc. Colallilo gave tremendous impetus to his company's attack, killed or wounded 25 of the enemy in bitter fighting, and assisted a wounded soldier in reaching the American lines at great risk of his own life.

Charles H. Coolidge
U.S. Army • WWII

"My creed and formula for successful living is simple. It sustained me through World War II: Trust not in thine own self but put your faith in Almighty God, and He will see you through. I had this brought home to me in vivid fashion on Hill 623 in southern France during WWII. Although faced with possible annihilation by an enemy force of greater numbers, my small body of brave soldiers overcame these overwhelming odds.

"Hill 623 in southern France will remain steadfast in my memory. The action that occurred there resulted in my being awarded the Medal of Honor, which is our country's highest military decoration. But I must be quick to state that the act that took place on a hill at Calvary far exceeds any victory that man can conceive. It was there that the Lord laid down His life for all who would believe and accept His gift of grace. Through His resurrection, victory over Satan was wrought and the plan of salvation became a living truth.

"For young people, I recommend that they set their priorities straight. Put God first in all things, and the remaining issues will fall in line. Simply conduct oneself in such a manner that if Christ should suddenly appear, personal behavior would prove no embarrassment to Him or to oneself. Be honest in all dealings with other people and share the love of Christ with whomever you find oppressed or despondent. And, finally, to thine own self be true lest you prove false to your fellow men. This is something that has sustained me through the trials of battle and the troublesome encounters of civilian life."

———◆•••◆———

Rank and organization
Technical Sergeant, U.S. Army, Company M,
141st Infantry, 36th Infantry Division.
Place and date
East of Belmont sur Buttant, France, 24-27 October 1944.

CITATION

Leading a section of heavy machineguns supported by 1 platoon of Company K, he took a position near Hill 623, east of Belmont sur Buttant, France, on 24 October 1944, with the mission of covering the right flank of the 3d Battalion and supporting its action. T/Sgt. Coolidge went forward with a sergeant of Company K to reconnoiter positions for coordinating the fires of the light and heavy machineguns.

They ran into an enemy force in the woods estimated to be an infantry company. T/Sgt. Coolidge, attempting to bluff the Germans by a show of assurance and boldness called upon them to surrender, whereupon the enemy opened fire. With his carbine, T/Sgt. Coolidge wounded two of them. There being no officer present with the force, T/Sgt. Coolidge at once assumed command. Many of the men were replacements recently arrived; this was their first experience under fire. T/Sgt. Coolidge, unmindful of the enemy fire delivered at close range, walked along the position, calming and encouraging his men and directing their fire. The attack was thrown back.

Through 25 and 26 October the enemy launched repeated attacks against the position of this combat group, but each was repulsed due to T/Sgt. Coolidge's able leadership. On 27 October, German infantry, supported by 2 tanks, made a determined attack on the position. The area was swept by enemy small arms, machinegun, and tank fire. T/Sgt. Coolidge armed himself with a bazooka and advanced to within 25 yards of the tanks. His bazooka failed to function and he threw it aside. Securing all the hand grenades he could carry, he crawled forward and inflicted heavy casualties on the advancing enemy. Finally it became apparent that the enemy, in greatly superior force, supported by tanks, would overrun the position. T/Sgt. Coolidge, displaying great coolness and courage, directed and conducted an orderly withdrawal, being himself the last to leave the position.

As a result of T/Sgt. Coolidge's heroic and superior leadership, the mission of this combat group was accomplished throughout four days of continuous fighting against numerically superior enemy troops in rain and cold and amid dense woods.

SHADOW OF DEATH – FEAR NOT

Ever since the fall of Adam, man has struggled to live in peace on this planet. The entry of Satan has wrought havoc on men and nations alike. Fierce battles have been fought to prevent world domination by satanic powers. Unfortunately, man has not solved this ongoing dilemma, and the threat of war still exists.

As I survey my military combat experience during World War II, I am confident that it was my strong Christian faith that sustained me during fierce battles. I held to the firm belief to trust not in thine ownself, but place your faith in Almighty God and He will see you through. On Hill 623, in Southern France during that global war, although faced with possible annihilation by a numerically superior enemy force, I did not fear the enemy who sought to overwhelm me on the field of battle.

Never did personal fear enter the situation. I kept remembering the words of my pastor back home. When I was a boy, he would recite the Bible story of David and Goliath and others who faced tremendous odds. I knew that same supernatural power was available to those who believed and remained faithful to God's commands. These memories helped to sustain me.

My sense of security was derived from the Christian training afforded me by my parents. Blessed with a godly mother who served as a Sunday School superintendent, and by a devout father who planted country churches and preached at missions stations, I possessed a protective blanket from caring parents whose chief interest was serving the Lord. It naturally followed that I would be the beneficiary of their petitioning prayers, particularly during my military service.

I served twenty months in combat, with 133 consecutive days of contact with the enemy (a World War II record). It is a miracle of God's grace and care that I received no wounds or injuries and returned home safely after front-line fighting through North Africa, Italy, France, Germany, and Austria. I give God the praise and the glory for His protection.

The Lord laid down His life for all who would believe and accept His gift of grace. Through His resurrection, victory over Satan was won and the plan of salvation became a living truth. That is victory in its highest form.

—*Charles Coolidge*

Master Sergeant William J. Crawford
U.S. Army (Ret.) • WWII

"Be the best of whatever you are. I read this poem in a USO library reading room in Algeria. As a Private, the poem made me feel worthwhile.

> If you can't be a moon, then just be a star
> But be the best of whatever you are.

"In a flank attack on the German main line of defense on the morning of September 13th, 1944, near Altavilla, Italy, several men near me were shot. I was untouched for some unknown reason. The Lord was looking after me. I accepted the Lord at Stalag IIB in Hammerstein, Germany, in September of 1944. At the time, Stalag IIB had received Bibles, hymnals, and an accordion. We organized a "Born Again" evangelistic-type of worship service. Having prayer services every day, more of the POWs accepted the Lord. A German officer escorted us out of the prison compound to a large meeting hall in Hammerstein. We had to give this up when the Russian army came through Poland. We had to march westward to escape the Russians, but we were liberated by the American army after marching for 52 days and 500 miles on a ration of one or two potatoes per night. I carried my Bible on my back and my New Testament in my left shirt pocket. How I survived, only the Lord knows."

Rank and organization
Private, U.S. Army, 36th Infantry Division.
Place and date
Near Altavilla, Italy, 13 September 1943.

CITATION

For conspicuous gallantry and intrepidity at risk of life above and beyond the call of duty in action with the enemy near Altavilla, Italy, 13 September 1943.

When Company I attacked an enemy-held position on Hill 424, the 3d Platoon, in which Pvt. Crawford was a squad scout, attacked as base platoon for the company. After reaching the crest of the hill, the platoon was pinned down by intense enemy machinegun and small-arms fire. Locating one of these guns, which was dug in on a terrace on his immediate front, Pvt. Crawford, without orders and on his own initiative, moved over the hill under enemy fire to a point within a few yards of the gun emplacement and single-handedly destroyed the machinegun and killed three of the crew with a hand grenade, thus enabling his platoon to continue its advance.

When the platoon, after reaching the crest, was once more delayed by enemy fire, Pvt. Crawford again, in the face of intense fire, advanced directly to the front midway between 2 hostile machinegun nests located on a higher terrace and emplaced in a small ravine. Moving first to the left, with a hand grenade he destroyed one gun emplacement and killed the crew; he then worked his way, under continuous fire, to the other and with one grenade and the use of his rifle, killed one enemy and forced the remainder to flee. Seizing the enemy machinegun, he fired on the withdrawing Germans and facilitated his company's advance.

John R. Crews
U.S. Army • WWII

"The statements below have hung on an 18" x 24" chalkboard in my bedroom for many years. This is a daily motivating reminder in all areas of my life. Each statement plays a different role in circumstances whether good or bad, large or small, great or uneventful: 'God only is great!' and 'Mind over matter.'

"Just a reminder, consider these things. What shall I do? None of the secrets of success work unless you do."

Rank and organization
Staff Sergeant, U.S. Army, Company F,
253d Infantry, 63d Infantry Division.
Place and date
Near Lobenbacherhof, Germany, 8 April 1945.

CITATION

He displayed conspicuous gallantry and intrepidity at the risk of his life above and beyond the call of duty on 8 April 1945 near Lobenbacherhof, Germany.

As his company was advancing toward the village under heavy fire, an enemy machinegun and automatic rifle with rifle support opened upon it from a hill on the right flank. Seeing that his platoon leader had been wounded by their fire, S/Sgt. Crews, acting on his own initiative, rushed the strongpoint with two men of his platoon. Despite the fact that one of these men was killed and the other was badly wounded, he continued his advance up the hill in the face of terrific enemy fire.

Storming the well-dug-in position single-handedly, he killed 2 of the crew of the machinegun at pointblank range with his M1 rifle and wrested the gun from the hands of the German whom he had already wounded. He then, with his rifle, charged the strongly emplaced automatic rifle. Although badly wounded in the thigh by crossfire from the remaining enemy, he kept on and silenced the entire position with his accurate and deadly rifle fire. His actions so unnerved the remaining enemy soldiers that 7 of them surrendered and the others fled.

His heroism caused the enemy to concentrate on him and permitted the company to move forward into the village.

Francis S. Currey
U.S. Army • WWII

"There are two groups of people: those who get things done, and those who take credit for getting things done. Belong to the first group. There is much less competition."

Rank and organization
Sergeant, U.S. Army, Company K, 120th Infantry,
30th Infantry Division.
Place and date
Malmedy, Belgium, 21 December 1944.

CITATION

He was an automatic rifleman with the 3d Platoon defending a strong point near Malmedy, Belgium, on 21 December 1944, when the enemy launched a powerful attack. Overrunning tank destroyers and antitank guns located near the strong point, German tanks advanced to the 3d Platoon's position, and, after prolonged fighting, forced the withdrawal of this group to a nearby factory.

Sgt. Currey found a bazooka in the building and crossed the street to secure rockets, meanwhile enduring intense fire from enemy tanks and hostile infantrymen who had taken up a position at a house a short distance away. In the face of small-arms, machinegun, and artillery fire, along with a companion, he knocked out a tank with one shot.

Moving to another position, he observed three Germans in the doorway of an enemy-held house. He killed or wounded all three with his automatic rifle. He emerged from cover and advanced alone to within 50 yards of the house, intent on wrecking it with rockets. Covered by friendly fire, he stood erect and fired a shot which knocked down half of one wall. While in this forward position, he observed five Americans who had been pinned down for hours by fire from the house and three tanks. Realizing that they could not escape until the enemy tank and infantry guns had been silenced, Sgt. Currey crossed the street to a vehicle, where he procured an armful of antitank grenades. These he launched while under heavy enemy fire, driving the tankmen from the vehicles into the house. He then climbed onto a half-track in full view of the Germans and fired a machinegun at the house.

Once again changing his position, he manned another machinegun whose crew had been killed; under his covering fire the five soldiers were able to retire to safety. Deprived of tanks and with heavy infantry casualties, the enemy was forced to withdraw.

Through his extensive knowledge of weapons and by his heroic and repeated braving of murderous enemy fire, Sgt. Currey was greatly responsible for inflicting heavy losses in men and material on the enemy, for rescuing five comrades, two of whom were wounded, and for stemming an attack which threatened to flank his battalion's position.

Michael J. Daly
U.S. Army • WWII

"Remember the Killed-in-Action, our truest heroes. Pray each morning that God will give you the strength, courage, and grace to do what is right. Assist the less fortunate.

"When the smoke has cleared from the last battlefield, and it will, we will stand there face to face with our own intact humanity and our own overwhelming need to help and respect one another."

Rank and organization
Captain (then Lieutenant), U.S. Army, Company A,
15th Infantry, 3d Infantry Division.
Place and date
Nuremberg, Germany, 18 April 1945. Entered service at:
Southport, Conn.

CITATION

Early in the morning of 18 April 1945, he led his company through the shell-battered, sniper-infested wreckage of Nuremberg, Germany. When blistering machinegun fire caught his unit in an exposed position, he ordered his men to take cover, dashed forward alone, and, as bullets whined about him, shot the 3-man guncrew with his carbine. Continuing the advance at the head of his company, he located an enemy patrol armed with rocket launchers which threatened friendly armor. He again went forward alone, secured a vantage point and opened fire on the Germans. Immediately he became the target for concentrated machine pistol and rocket fire, which blasted the rubble about him. Calmly, he continued to shoot at the patrol until he had killed all 6 enemy infantrymen.

Continuing boldly far in front of his company, he entered a park, where as his men advanced, a German machinegun opened up on them without warning. With his carbine, he killed the gunner; and then, from a completely exposed position, he directed machinegun fire on the remainder of the crew until all were dead. In a final duel, he wiped out a third machinegun emplacement with rifle fire at a range of 10 yards. By fearlessly engaging in 4 single-handed firefights with a desperate, powerfully armed enemy, Lt. Daly, voluntarily taking all major risks himself and protecting his men at every opportunity, killed 15 Germans, silenced 3 enemy machineguns, and wiped out an entire enemy patrol.

His heroism during the lone bitter struggle with fanatical enemy forces was an inspiration to the valiant Americans who took Nuremberg.

General Raymond G. Davis
U.S. Marine Corps (Ret.) • Korea

"Two leadership ideas always come to mind. I have shared them with many, many young officers. As you take care of your Marines, so will they take care of you. Never concentrate on getting good jobs, but instead, go all out and give your very best in the job you have."

Rank and organization
Lieutenant Colonel, U.S. Marine Corps commanding officer, 1st Battalion, 7th Marines, 1st Marine Division (Rein.).
Place and date
Vicinity Hagaru-ri, Korea, 1 through 4 December 1950.

CITATION
For conspicuous gallantry and intrepidity at the risk of his life above and beyond the call of duty as commanding officer of the 1st Battalion, in action against enemy aggressor forces.

Although keenly aware that the operation involved breaking through a surrounding enemy and advancing eight miles along primitive icy trails in the bitter cold with every passage disputed by a savage and determined foe, Lt. Col. Davis boldly led his battalion into the attack in a daring attempt to relieve a beleaguered rifle company and to seize, hold, and defend a vital mountain pass controlling the only route available for two marine regiments in danger of being cut off by numerically superior hostile forces during their re-deployment to the port of Hungnam.

When the battalion immediately encountered strong opposition from entrenched enemy forces commanding high ground in the path of the advance, he promptly spearheaded his unit in a fierce attack up the steep, ice-covered slopes in the face of withering fire and, personally leading the assault groups in a hand-to-hand encounter, drove the hostile troops from their positions, rested his men, and reconnoitered the area under enemy fire to determine the best route for continuing the mission.

Always in the thick of the fighting Lt. Col. Davis led his battalion over three successive ridges in the deep snow in continuous attacks against the enemy and, constantly inspiring and encouraging his men throughout the night, brought his unit to a point within 1,500 yards of the surrounded rifle company by daybreak. Although knocked to the ground when a shell fragment struck his helmet and two bullets pierced his clothing, he arose and fought his way forward at the head of his men until he reached the isolated marines. On the following morning, he bravely led his battalion in securing the vital mountain pass from a strongly entrenched and numerically superior hostile force, carrying all his wounded with him, including 22 litter cases and numerous ambulatory patients.

Despite repeated savage and heavy assaults by the enemy, he stubbornly held the vital terrain until the two regiments of the division had deployed through the pass and, on the morning of 4 December, led his battalion into Hagaru-ri intact.

By his superb leadership, outstanding courage, and brilliant tactical ability, Lt. Col. Davis was directly instrumental in saving the beleaguered rifle company from complete annihilation and enabled the two marine regiments to escape possible destruction. His valiant devotion to duty and unyielding fighting spirit in the face of almost insurmountable odds enhance and sustain the highest traditions of the U.S. Naval Service.

Sammy L. Davis
U.S. Army • Vietnam

"DUTY...HONOR...COUNTRY: these words were spoken by General Douglas McArthur so long ago. I took them to heart and have tried to live my life by that code. Though I have been called a hero for the action I took in combat in Vietnam, I know through my own experiences that a man who is willing to die for his country is dedicated, and a man who endeavors to live for his country is committed. I truly pray that those who hear me speak, as I do at various functions around the country, will leave remembering just that.

"If you are willing to live for your country, to make that kind of commitment, you are the heroes that will help America fulfill its promise. A lifelong devotion to duty, honor, and country by men and women throughout our history has nourished the cause of freedom. As we pass the torch from generation to generation, it is imperative that we pass on the understanding of the work it takes to perpetuate the promise. Liberty offers us boundless opportunity. Those opportunities will cease to exist if we forget to continue as vanguards of our freedom. As difficult as the task may be, if we face each new day with a resolve to live for our country, and follow the dictum of duty, honor, and country, America will grow greater and stronger and more bountiful with the passing of each day. I believe we can achieve everything of real importance through these three words."

Sergeant, U.S. Army, Battery C, 2d Battalion,
4th Artillery, 9th Infantry Division.
Place and date
West of Cai Lay, Republic of Vietnam, 18 November 1967.

CITATION

For conspicuous gallantry and intrepidity in action at the risk of his life and beyond the call of duty. Sgt. Davis (then Pfc.) distinguished himself during the early morning hours while serving as a cannoneer with Battery C, at a remote fire support base.

At approximately 0200 hours, the fire support base was under heavy enemy mortar attack. Simultaneously, an estimated reinforced Viet Cong battalion launched a fierce ground assault upon the fire support base. The attacking enemy drove to within 25 meters of the friendly positions. Only a river separated the Viet Cong from the fire support base. Detecting a nearby enemy position, Sgt. Davis seized a machine gun and provided covering fire for his guncrew, as they attempted to bring direct artillery fire on the enemy. Despite his efforts, an enemy recoilless rifle round scored a direct hit upon the artillery piece. The resultant blast hurled the guncrew from their weapon and blew Sgt. Davis into a foxhole.

He struggled to his feet and returned to the howitzer, which was burning furiously. Ignoring repeated warnings to seek cover, Sgt. Davis rammed a shell into the gun. Disregarding a withering hail of enemy fire directed against his position, he aimed and fired the howitzer which rolled backward, knocking Sgt. Davis violently to the ground. Undaunted, he returned to the weapon to fire again when an enemy mortar round exploded within 20 meters of his position, injuring him painfully. Nevertheless, Sgt. Davis loaded the artillery piece, aimed and fired. Again he was knocked down by the recoil. In complete disregard for his safety, Sgt. Davis loaded and fired three more shells into the enemy.

Disregarding his extensive injuries and his inability to swim, Sgt. Davis picked up an air mattress and struck out across the deep river to rescue three wounded comrades on the far side. Upon reaching the three wounded men, he stood upright and fired into the dense vegetation to prevent the Viet Cong from advancing. While the most seriously wounded soldier was helped across the river, Sgt. Davis protected the two remaining casualties until he could pull them across the river to the fire support base. Though suffering from painful wounds, he refused medical attention, joining another howitzer crew which fired at the large Viet Cong force until it broke contact and fled.

Sgt. Davis' extraordinary heroism, at the risk of his life, are in keeping with the highest traditions of the military service and reflect great credit upon himself and the U.S. Army.

"I would rather have the blue band of the Medal of Honor around my neck than be President."
                              —*Harry S Truman*

"A people that have forgotten their heritage are a people who have lost faith in themselves."
                              —*Winston S. Churchill*

"Let every nation know, whether it wishes us well or ill, that we shall pay any price, bear any burden, meet any hardship, support any friend, oppose any foe, in order to assure the survival and the success of liberty."
                              —*John F. Kennedy*

Colonel George "Bud" E. Day
U.S. Air Force (Ret.) • Vietnam

"Every one needs a role model—an individual who will make you a better person and a better citizen. Perhaps the best role model would be Jesus Christ. He taught us to lead, by teaching us how to follow. He gave us standards to live by, called the Ten Commandments. When asked what is the greatest commandment, He said to love God and love your neighbor as yourself. Living out these standards will never put you on the wrong side of any problem."

Rank and organization
Colonel (then Major), U.S. Air Force, Forward
Air Controller Pilot of an F-100 aircraft.
Place and date
North Vietnam, 26 August 1967.

CITATION

On 26 August 1967, Col. Day was forced to eject from his aircraft over North Vietnam when it was hit by ground fire. His right arm was broken in 3 places, and his left knee was badly sprained. He was immediately captured by hostile forces and taken to a prison camp where he was interrogated and severely tortured. After causing the guards to relax their vigilance, Col. Day escaped into the jungle and began the trek toward South Vietnam. Despite injuries inflicted by fragments of a bomb or rocket, he continued southward surviving only on a few berries and uncooked frogs. He successfully evaded enemy patrols and reached the Ben Hai River, where he encountered U.S. artillery barrages. With the aid of a bamboo log float, Col. Day swam across the river and entered the demilitarized zone. Due to delirium, he lost his sense of direction and wandered aimlessly for several days.

After several unsuccessful attempts to signal U.S. aircraft, he was ambushed and recaptured by the Viet Cong, sustaining gunshot wounds to his left hand and thigh. He was returned to the prison from which he had escaped and later was moved to Hanoi after giving his captors false information to questions put before him. Physically, Col. Day was totally debilitated and unable to perform even the simplest task for himself. Despite his many injuries, he continued to offer maximum resistance. His personal bravery in the face of deadly enemy pressure was significant in saving the lives of fellow aviators who were still flying against the enemy.

Col. Day's conspicuous gallantry and intrepidity at the risk of his life above and beyond the call of duty are in keeping with the highest traditions of the U.S. Air Force and reflect great credit upon himself and the U.S. Armed Forces.

Colonel Jefferson DeBlanc
U.S. Marine Corps (Ret.) WWII

"I always stress TRUTH, a POSITIVE ATTITUDE, and NEVER JUDGE your fellow men! I learned early in combat that the Lord saved my life for some reason. Three times I went through experiences which left me wondering why I survived; there had to be a reason. When I went through the Okinawa campaign, it was revealed to me in strong terms.

"I was to lead a flight of 90 fighters for a strike on the Japanese island of Ishigaki. Since it was close to the end of the war and Zero fighters were not too active, we were given a new type of 500 lb. bomb with a VT-fuse to carry on this flight. The General said in his briefing NOT to drop the bomb without getting on target. This was to prevent the Japanese from getting this 'new' radio control fuse detonator. I was a little apprehensive about taking this flight since we did not have any pre-planning with this type of weapon. I was assigned a different fighter from the one I usually flew, and 20 minutes into the flight, four of our planes blew up. The cause was faulty wiring to ground the nose pin which kept the fuse detonator from being activated during the flight. The pins pulled out due to wind action since they were not wired inline with the flight path of the aircraft. Needless to say, one of the fighters was the aircraft I usually flew."

Rank and Organization
Captain, U.S. Marine Corps Reserve,
Marine Fighting Squadron 112.
Place and date
Off Kolombangara Island in the Solomons group, 1/31/43.

CITATION

For conspicuous gallantry and intrepidity at the risk of his life above and beyond the call of duty as leader of a section of six fighter planes in Marine Fighting Squadron 112, during aerial operations against enemy Japanese forces off Kolombangara Island in the Solomons group, 31 January 1943.

Taking off with his section as escort for a strike force of dive bombers and torpedo planes ordered to attack Japanese surface vessels, 1st Lt. DeBlanc led his flight directly to the target area where, at 14,000 feet, our strike force encountered a large number of Japanese Zeros protecting the enemy's surface craft. In company with the other fighters, 1st Lt. DeBlanc instantly engaged the hostile planes and aggressively countered their repeated attempts to drive off our bombers, persevering in his efforts to protect the diving planes and waging fierce combat until, picking up a call for assistance from the dive bombers under attack by enemy float planes at 1,000 feet, he broke off his engagement with the Zeros, plunged into the formation of float planes and disrupted the savage attack, enabling our dive bombers and torpedo planes to complete their runs on the Japanese surface disposition and withdraw without further incident.

Although his escort mission was fulfilled upon the safe retirement of the bombers, 1st Lt. DeBlanc courageously remained on the scene despite a rapidly diminishing fuel supply and, boldly challenging the enemy's superior number of float planes, fought a valiant battle against terrific odds, seizing the tactical advantage and striking repeatedly to destroy three of the hostile aircraft and to disperse the remainder. Prepared to maneuver his damaged plane back to base, he had climbed aloft and set his course when he discovered two Zeros closing in behind. Undaunted, he opened fire and blasted both Zeros from the sky in a short, bitterly fought action which resulted in such hopeless damage to his own plane that he was forced to bail out at a perilously low altitude atop the trees on enemy-held Kolombangara.

A gallant officer, a superb airman, and an indomitable fighter, 1st Lt. DeBlanc had rendered decisive assistance during a critical stage of operations, and his unwavering fortitude in the face of overwhelming opposition reflects the highest credit upon himself and adds new luster to the traditions of the U.S. Naval Service.

The Lord's Prayer

Our Father which art in heaven, Hallowed be thy name. Thy kingdom come. Thy will be done in earth, as it is in heaven. Give us this day our daily bread. And forgive us our debts, as we forgive our debtors. And lead us not into temptation, but deliver us from evil: For thine is the kingdom, and the power, and the glory, for ever. Amen (Matthew 6:9-13).

Duane E. Dewey
U.S. Marine Corps • Korea

"I don't often speak at schools or offer advice, but the advice I would offer is this: You need to like the job that you do, whatever it is. If you like your job, you will be successful. If you don't like your job, most likely you won't find success. In life it is important to never give up, be honest, and have faith in God."

Rank and organization
Corporal, U.S. Marine Corps Reserve, Company E,
2d Battalion, 5th Marines, 1st Marine Division (Rein.).
Place and date
Near Panmunjon, Korea, 16 April 1952.

CITATION

For conspicuous gallantry and intrepidity at the risk of his life above and beyond the call of duty while serving as a gunner in a machine gun platoon of Company E, in action against enemy aggressor forces.

When an enemy grenade landed close to his position while he and his assistant gunner were receiving medical attention for their wounds during a fierce night attack by numerically superior hostile forces, Cpl. Dewey, although suffering intense pain, immediately pulled the corpsman to the ground and, shouting a warning to the other marines around him, bravely smothered the deadly missile with his body, personally absorbing the full force of the explosion to save his comrades from possible injury or death.

His indomitable courage, outstanding initiative, and valiant efforts in behalf of others in the face of almost certain death reflect the highest credit upon Cpl. Dewey and enhance the finest traditions of the U.S. Naval Service.

Major Drew D. Dix
U.S. Army (Ret.) • Vietnam

"The tremendous honor of being decorated by the President of the United States is completely overshadowed by the humbling realization of being recommended for the Medal of Honor by fellow warriors. My advice for anyone undertaking a difficult profession or experience is: Never give up. Hard work and persistence are important. You will be surprised—nothing is ever as hard as you think it might be."

Rank and Organization
Staff Sergeant, U.S. Army, U.S. Senior Advisor Group, IV Corps, Military Assistance Command.
Place and date
Chau Doc Province, Republic of Vietnam, 31 January and 1 February 1968.

CITATION
For conspicuous gallantry and intrepidity in action at the risk of his life above and beyond the call of duty. S/Sgt. Dix distinguished himself by exceptional heroism while serving as a unit adviser.

Two heavily armed Viet Cong battalions attacked the Province capital city of Chau Phu resulting in the complete breakdown and fragmentation of the defenses of the city. S/Sgt. Dix, with a patrol of Vietnamese soldiers, was recalled to assist in the defense of Chau Phu. Learning that a nurse was trapped in a house near the center of the city, S/Sgt. Dix organized a relief force, successfully rescued the nurse and returned her to the safety of the Tactical Operations Center. Being informed of other trapped civilians within the city, S/Sgt. Dix voluntarily led another force to rescue 8 civilian employees located in a building which was under heavy mortar and small-arms fire. S/Sgt. Dix then returned to the center of the city. Upon approaching a building, he was subjected to intense automatic rifle and machine gun fire from an unknown number of Viet Cong. He personally assaulted the building, killing 6 Viet Cong, and rescuing 2 Filipinos.

The following day S/Sgt. Dix, still on his own volition, assembled a 20-man force and, though under intense enemy fire, cleared the Viet Cong out of the hotel, theater, and other adjacent buildings within the city. During this portion of the attack, Army Republic of Vietnam soldiers, inspired by the heroism and success of S/Sgt. Dix, rallied and commenced firing upon the Viet Cong. S/Sgt. Dix captured 20 prisoners, including a high ranking Viet Cong official. He then attacked enemy troops who had entered the residence of the Deputy Province Chief and was successful in rescuing the official's wife and children. S/Sgt. Dix's personal heroic actions resulted in 14 confirmed Viet Cong killed in action and possibly 25 more, the capture of 20 prisoners, 15 weapons, and the rescue of the 14 United States and free world civilians.

The heroism of S/Sgt. Dix was in the highest tradition and reflects great credit upon the U.S. Army.

Colonel Roger H.C. Donlon
U.S. Army (Ret.) • Vietnam

"I have found that LISTENING is one of the purest ways of praying. I also have found it helpful to constantly remind myself that what we are is God's gift to us; what we become is our gift to God."

Rank and organization
Captain, U.S. Army.
Place and date
Near Nam Dong, Republic of Vietnam, 6 July 1964.

CITATION

For conspicuous gallantry and intrepidity at the risk of his life above and beyond the call of duty while defending a U.S. military installation against a fierce attack by hostile forces.

Capt. Donlon was serving as the commanding officer of the U.S. Army Special Forces Detachment A-726 at Camp Nam Dong when a reinforced Viet Cong battalion suddenly launched a full-scale, predawn attack on the camp. During the violent battle that ensued, lasting five hours and resulting in heavy casualties on both sides, Capt. Donlon directed the defense operations in the midst of an enemy barrage of mortar shells, falling grenades, and extremely heavy gunfire.

Upon the initial onslaught, he swiftly marshaled his forces and ordered the removal of the needed ammunition from a blazing building. He then dashed through a hail of small arms and exploding hand grenades to abort a breach of the main gate. En route to this position, he detected an enemy demolition team of three in the proximity of the main gate and quickly annihilated them. Although exposed to the intense grenade attack, he then succeeded in reaching a 60mm mortar position despite sustaining a severe stomach wound as he was within five yards of the gun pit. When he discovered that most of the men in this gunpit were also wounded, he completely disregarded his own injury, directed their withdrawal to a location 30 meters away, and again risked his life by remaining behind and covering the movement with the utmost effectiveness.

Noticing that his team sergeant was unable to evacuate the gun pit, he crawled toward him and, while he was dragging the fallen soldier out of the gunpit, an enemy mortar exploded and inflicted a wound in Capt. Donlon's left shoulder. Although suffering from multiple wounds, he carried the abandoned 60mm mortar weapon to a new location 30 meters away where he found three wounded defenders. After administering first aid and encouragement to these men, he left the weapon with them, headed toward another position, and retrieved a 57mm recoilless rifle.

Then with great courage and coolness under fire, he returned to the abandoned gun pit, evacuated ammunition for the two weapons, and while crawling and dragging the urgently needed ammunition, received a third wound on his leg by an enemy hand grenade. Despite his critical physical condition, he again crawled 175 meters to an 81mm mortar position and directed firing operations which protected the seriously threatened east sector of the camp. He then moved to an eastern 60mm mortar position and upon determining that the vicious enemy assault had weakened, crawled back to the gun pit with the 60mm mortar, set it up for defensive operations, and turned it over to two defenders with minor wounds.

Without hesitation, he left this sheltered position, and moved from position to position around the beleaguered perimeter while hurling hand grenades at the enemy and inspiring his men to superhuman effort. As he bravely continued to move around the perimeter, a mortar shell exploded, wounding him in the face and body. As the long awaited daylight brought defeat to the enemy forces and their retreat back to the jungle leaving behind 54 of their dead, many weapons, and grenades, Capt. Donlon immediately reorganized his defenses and administered first aid to the wounded.

His dynamic leadership, fortitude, and valiant efforts inspired not only the American personnel but the friendly Vietnamese defenders as well and resulted in the successful defense of the camp. Capt. Donlon's extraordinary heroism, at the risk of his life above and beyond the call of duty are in the highest traditions of the U.S. Army and reflect great credit upon himself and the Armed Forces of his country.

Refinement of MOH Awards

The Medal of Honor was created in 1862, but it was the act of 9 July 1918 that defined the future of the award, while further eliminating the Certificate of Merit and establishing the new "Pyramid of Honor," which provided for lesser awards (The Distinguished Service Cross, The Distinguished Service Medal, and the Silver Star). A key difference between the levels of awards was spelled out, "That the President is authorized to present, in the name of the Congress, a medal of honor only to each person who, while an officer or enlisted man of the Army, shall hereafter, in action involving actual conflict with an enemy, distinguish himself conspicuously by gallantry and intrepidity at the risk of his life above and beyond the call of duty."

The act of July 9th was further clarified in September, then again in February 1919, to stipulate that no person could receive more than ONE Medal of Honor. Previously there had been 19 DOUBLE AWARDS of the Medal, but hereafter, while there were provisions for second and consecutive awards of lesser medals to be made and noted with appropriate ribbon devices, no more than ONE Medal of Honor could be awarded.

Desmond T. Doss
U.S. Army WWII

"I would like to share my godly mother's advice: Live by the Golden Rule and do unto others as you would have them do unto you. Study the Bible daily, for it is God's love letter to us letting us know right from wrong; it is our road map to heaven. He has not asked us to give up anything good, only that which is not good enough for life eternal with Him and our loved ones. Eye hath not seen nor ear heard, neither hath it entered into the heart of man the wonderful things He has gone to prepare for us who love Him and keep His holy law. If we miss heaven, we have missed everything."

Rank and organization
Private First Class, U.S. Army, Medical Detachment,
307th Infantry, 77th Infantry Division.
Place and date
Near Urasoe Mura, Okinawa, Ryukyu Islands, 4/29–5/21/45.

CITATION

He was a company aid man when the 1st Battalion assaulted a jagged escarpment 400 feet high. As our troops gained the summit, a heavy concentration of artillery, mortar and machinegun fire crashed into them, inflicting approximately 75 casualties and driving the others back. Pfc. Doss refused to seek cover and remained in the fire-swept area with the many stricken, carrying them one by one to the edge of the escarpment and there lowering them on a rope-supported litter down the face of a cliff to friendly hands.

On 2 May, he exposed himself to heavy rifle and mortar fire in rescuing a wounded man 200 yards forward of the lines on the same escarpment; and two days later he treated four men who had been cut down while assaulting a strongly defended cave, advancing through a shower of grenades to within eight yards of enemy forces in a cave's mouth, where he dressed his comrades' wounds before making four separate trips under fire to evacuate them to safety.

On 5 May, he unhesitatingly braved enemy shelling and small arms fire to assist an artillery officer. He applied bandages, moved his patient to a spot that offered protection from small arms fire and, while artillery and mortar shells fell close by, painstakingly administered plasma. Later that day, when an American was severely wounded by fire from a cave, Pfc. Doss crawled to him where he had fallen 25 feet from the enemy position, rendered aid, and carried him 100 yards to safety while continually exposed to enemy fire.

On 21 May, in a night attack on high ground near Shuri, he remained in exposed territory while the rest of his company took cover, fearlessly risking the chance that he would be mistaken for an infiltrating Japanese and giving aid to the injured until he was himself seriously wounded in the legs by the explosion of a grenade.

Rather than call another aid man from cover, he cared for his own injuries and waited five hours before litter bearers reached him and started carrying him to cover. The trio was caught in an enemy tank attack and Pfc. Doss, seeing a more critically wounded man nearby, crawled off the litter and directed the bearers to give their first attention to the other man. Awaiting the litter bearers' return, he was again struck, this time suffering a compound fracture of one arm. With magnificent fortitude he bound a rifle stock to his shattered arm as a splint and then crawled 300 yards over rough terrain to the aid station.

Through his outstanding bravery and unflinching determination in the face of desperately dangerous conditions, Pfc. Doss saved the lives of many soldiers. His name became a symbol throughout the 77th Infantry Division for outstanding gallantry far above and beyond the call of duty.

MIRACLE DAY

On the island of Okinawa in the Pacific is a big hill called the Maeda Escarpment. It is a hill that goes up gradually on one side, levels off on top and then drops off 400 feet to the valley below. During World War II, the American army was in the valley below the 400 foot drop off. It wasn't easy to get up the cliff the first 365 feet, but it was possible. But the last 35 feet was straight up and jutted out about five feet at the top.

I was a medic in B company attached to the 307th regiment of the 77th infantry division, the Statue of Liberty Division. We had fought on top of the escarpment for a number of days without much progress being made. The escarpment was honeycombed with caves and tunnels. The Japanese put ladders from one cave or tunnel to another on the inside of the escarpment. On top were foxholes that looked like natural terrain, making it easy for them to shoot Americans who didn't even know they were there.

As we prepared to go up on top of the escarpment again this particular day, I went to Lieutenant Gornto and suggested, "I believe prayer is the best life-saver there is." Immediately he called our group together and said, "Gather round, fellows. Doss wants to pray for us."

Now that was not what I had in mind. I just wanted to remind the men that none of us was sure of a return down the escarpment because we knew how fierce the fighting was, and that each man should pray for himself. But after the lieutenant said that, I did pray. I prayed that God would be with the lieutenant and help him to give us the correct orders as our lives were in his hands and help each one of us to take all the safety precautions necessary so that we could all come back alive.

With that we started up the escarpment and immediately got pinned down and thought we couldn't move. Shortly a message came through headquarters asking what our losses were. I answered, "None so far."

Again a message came through. "Company A who is fighting

on your left, has been so badly shot up, they can't do any more. Company B will have to take the whole escarpment by yourselves." How would you like to get orders like that? Uncle Sam has to sacrifice lives to take important objectives, and the Maeda Escarpment was a very important objective.

So we started to move forward. As I remember, Company B started to take enemy positions one at a time until we had taken eight or nine Japanese positions. The amazing part of it was that not a single man from Company B was killed and only one man was slightly wounded by a rock that hit his hand. That was one day that I, as a medic, didn't have much to do.

It was such an amazing happening that word began to get around to various companies, to headquarters and even back to the States. The men of Company B were asked, "How did you manage to do that?" Their answer, "Due to Doss' prayer." They recognized that God had cared for them in a very special way because of the prayer of protection.

The next day we were to go up on the escarpment again. We figured the work was done and this was just a mop-up job. I didn't pray and I doubt if anyone else did either. That day everything went wrong. The men would throw grenades and other high explosives and the Japanese would pull the fuses before they went off. A number of my men were wounded and needed help. Four men were together in a forward position. One of them tried to throw a grenade. It went off prematurely and he lost his hand. The other three were also wounded. I went to them, did a little first aid and then carried them back one-by-one to the edge of the escarpment.

There was one Japanese foxhole that was giving us trouble. In spite of all the ammunition our men directed into the foxhole, it was still active and in Japanese hands. Finally several of the men opened cans of high octane gasoline and literally threw the cans and the gas into the foxhole. I understand a lieutenant threw a white phosphorous grenade into the gasoline. The resulting explosion was much more than expected. All of the ammunition the men had thrown into the foxhole exploded, probably the Japanese ammunition dump down below went off, too.

What happened next was also unexpected. The Japanese evidently figured it was now or never, and they came at us from all sides. The command was given to retreat. Many of our men were wounded and remained on top of the escarpment. They were my men and I felt I could not leave them. I started to pull them to the edge, and one-by-one I began to let them down using a double bowline knot that I had worked with one time while still in the states. It made two loops that could be pulled over the feet and up the legs of the wounded soldiers. Then I would tie another bowline knot around their chest and let them down the first 35 feet to where they could be carried to the aid station. The Lord even provided a tree stump that I could wind rope around and let them down easy.

I kept praying, "Lord, help me get one more." The Lord answered my prayer. I was able to get all the men down that day. The army said it was 100, but I told them it couldn't be more than 50. So my citation for the Medal of Honor says 75.

On October 12th, 1945, President Truman presented me with the Congressional Medal of Honor. I believe that I received the Medal of Honor because I remembered to keep the Golden Rule as stated in Matthew 7:12, "Therefore all things whatsoever ye would that men should do to you, do ye even so to them."

—*Desmond T. Doss*

Major Robert H. Dunlap
U.S. Marine Corps (Ret.) • WWII

"I graduated from college early so I could join the Marine Corps. I received the Medal of Honor for action on Iwo Jima. During that battle, I was severely wounded by a Japanese sniper and ended up paralyzed in the hospital with a severe infection in my spine called osteomyelitis. The doctors told me I would never walk again. My sister, a physical therapist, and my fiancée decided to help with my therapy. Part of my treatment was to drink bone broth. I drank gallons and gallons of the stuff. For six months my sister and my wife-to-be helped with my physical therapy. At the end of six months, I was walking on my own.

"After I left the service I decided to farm and did so for 15 years. After a farming accident, I used my college degree and became a teacher. I was blessed to become a successful coach and teacher.

"The advice that I would give to young men and women is: Never give up, and always, always keep a positive attitude. Continue your education because it will allow you the opportunity to become a positive influence. Trust in God and have faith in Him. I believe my positive attitude, and God helping me with that attitude, enabled me not only to walk but also to have a positive affect on my family and the students I taught throughout my life."

Rank and organization
Captain, U.S. Marine Corps Reserve, Company C,
1st Battalion, 26th Marines, 5th Marine Division.
Place and date
On Iwo Jima, Volcano Islands, 20 and 21 February 1945.

CITATION

For conspicuous gallantry and intrepidity at the risk of his life above and beyond the call of duty as commanding officer of Company C, 1st Battalion, 26th Marines, 5th Marine Division, in action against enemy Japanese forces during the seizure of Iwo Jima in the Volcano Islands, on 20 and 21 February, 1945.

Defying uninterrupted blasts of Japanese artillery, mortar, rifle, and machinegun fire, Capt. Dunlap led his troops in a determined advance from low ground uphill toward the steep cliffs from which the enemy poured a devastating rain of shrapnel and bullets, steadily inching forward until the tremendous volume of enemy fire from the caves located high to his front temporarily halted his progress. Determined not to yield, he crawled alone approximately 200 yards forward of his front lines, took observation at the base of the cliff 50 yards from Japanese lines, located the enemy gun positions, and returned to his own lines where he relayed the vital information to supporting artillery and naval gunfire units. Persistently disregarding his own personal safety, he then placed himself in an exposed vantage point to direct more accurately the supporting fire and, working without respite for 2 days and 2 nights under constant enemy fire, skillfully directed a smashing bombardment against the almost impregnable Japanese positions despite numerous obstacles and heavy marine casualties.

A brilliant leader, Capt. Dunlap inspired his men to heroic efforts during this critical phase of the battle and by his cool decision, indomitable fighting spirit, and daring tactics in the face of fanatic opposition greatly accelerated the final decisive defeat of Japanese countermeasures in his sector and materially furthered the continued advance of his company. His great personal valor and gallant spirit of self-sacrifice throughout the bitter hostilities reflect the highest credit upon Capt. Dunlap and the U.S. Naval Service.

Walter D. Ehlers
U.S. Army • WWII

"When I enlisted in the United States Army, I had to get my dad's and mother's signatures. My dad had agreed to sign. My mother said, with tears in her eyes, 'I will sign if you promise to be a Christian soldier.' I assured her I would do my best. It wasn't easy being a Christian soldier, but each time I was tempted, I would see the tears in my mother's eyes and I would remember my promise.

"I also would realize I had made a commitment to God. I had no intention of dishonoring my mother and, above all, God. My faith in God, my fellow men, and myself, made the difference. This is why I am a survivor of the war. In order to have faith in yourself, you must arm yourself with complete knowledge of your job. Requirements include honesty, compassion, courage, education, faith, and commitment. I am not a saint, but my faith and determination to do my best worked for me."

Rank and organization
Staff Sergeant, U.S. Army, 18th Infantry, 1st Infantry Division.
Place and date
Near Goville, France, 9-10 June 1944.

CITATION

For conspicuous gallantry and intrepidity at the risk of his life above and beyond the call of duty on 9-10 June 1944, near Goville, France.

S/Sgt. Ehlers, always acting as the spearhead of the attack, repeatedly led his men against heavily defended enemy strong points exposing himself to deadly hostile fire whenever the situation required heroic and courageous leadership. Without waiting for an order, S/Sgt. Ehlers, far ahead of his men, led his squad against a strongly defended enemy strong point, personally killing 4 of an enemy patrol who attacked him en route. Then crawling forward under withering machinegun fire, he pounced upon the guncrew and put it out of action. Turning his attention to 2 mortars protected by the crossfire of 2 machineguns, S/Sgt. Ehlers led his men through this hail of bullets to kill or put to flight the enemy of the mortar section, killing 3 men himself. After mopping up the mortar positions, he again advanced on a machinegun, his progress effectively covered by his squad. When he was almost on top of the gun, he leaped to his feet and, although greatly outnumbered, he knocked out the position single-handed.

The next day, having advanced deep into enemy territory, the platoon of which S/Sgt. Ehlers was a member, finding itself in an untenable position as the enemy brought increased mortar, machinegun, and small arms fire to bear on it, was ordered to withdraw. S/Sgt. Ehlers, after his squad had covered the withdrawal of the remainder of the platoon, stood up and by continuous fire at the semicircle of enemy placements, diverted the bulk of the heavy hostile fire on himself, thus permitting the members of his own squad to withdraw. At this point, though wounded himself, he carried his wounded automatic rifleman to safety and then returned fearlessly over the shell-swept field to retrieve the automatic rifle which he was unable to carry previously. After having his wound treated, he refused to be evacuated, and returned to lead his squad.

The intrepid leadership, indomitable courage, and fearless aggressiveness displayed by S/Sgt. Ehlers in the face of overwhelming enemy forces serve as an inspiration to others.

———

THE PRAYERS OF A MOTHER

I grew up on a farm near Manhattan, Kansas. My oldest brother, Roland, and I both enlisted at the same time and began our training at Fort Lewis, Washington. When we found out we were going to North Africa, we were in the same Infantry company. We landed at Casablanca and were together during the North Africa campaign, and we were together again in Sicily. Roland was wounded in Sicily and was sent back to Africa to recover, but we were together again in England before the Normandy Invasion on D-Day. Because of the danger, our company Commander decided to put us in different companies prior to the invasion.

On D-Day, my landing craft dropped us off in water so deep that it was over our heads. When we finally made it to the beach, the men wanted to lie down. I told them we had to get off the beach or we would all be killed. We made our way up a steep hill and knocked out a bunker. This allowed us to get off the beach. Over the next few days I tried to find out about Roland, but he was declared Missing-In-Action. It was over a month before I finally received the news that he had been killed on the beach when his landing craft was hit by mortar or artillery fire.

Within a few days my squad was involved in fierce fighting. It was because of this action that the men in my squad requested that I receive the Medal of Honor. During the firefight, I was wounded by an enemy sniper. The bullet struck me in the ribs and went around to my back and into my backpack. The bullet tore through the pack and struck the edge of my mother's picture.

During the war I carried and read my pocket New Testament

that included the Psalms. I found great comfort in reading the twenty-third Psalm and the Lord's Prayer. I also found great comfort knowing that my family, and especially my mother, were praying for me. In every letter I received from my mother, she told me she was praying for me and for my two brothers. She had three sons in the war.

I guess my New Testament must have been lost when I was wounded. About ten years after the war, it arrived in the mail. A German lady sent it to my mother because her name and address were written in the front pages of the Bible. Apparently the woman's children found the Bible under some rocks behind their home. The lady, not knowing if I survived the war, said she wanted to send the Bible, hoping that it would comfort my mother. Mom was thrilled to receive it, but she was just as excited to realize that it was worn from my reading it during the war. She realized that I had tried to be a Christian soldier. My mother was an inspiration to me and to our family. Where would we be without mothers that pray for us?

—*Walter Ehlers*

Henry E. Erwin
U.S. Army Air Corps • WWII

"On April 19th, 1945, the Medal of Honor was flown from Hawaii to Fleet Hospital 103, Guam, to be given to me on my death bed. General LeMay had recommended the award, and it was approved in record time.

"With time, I was moved to within 50 miles of my home. I was hospitalized for two-and-one-half years. I have had 43 plastic surgeries for the burns and severe injuries I received on that fateful day in 1945.

"While in the hospital I was visited by Miss Helen Keller and her friend Polly Thompson. Her wonderful attitude and excitement were two things that I never forgot. She was such an inspiration to me and all of the other wounded veterans. I still remember the letter she wrote to me and the way she signed it in block letters.

"My code for life is: Never give up, and treat others as you would have them treat you."

Rank and organization
Staff Sergeant, U.S. Army Air Corps, 52d Bombardment Squadron, 29th Bombardment Group, 20th Air Force.
Place and date
Koriyama, Japan, 12 April 1945.

CITATION

He was the radio operator of a B-29 airplane leading a group formation to attack Koriyama, Japan. He was charged with the additional duty of dropping phosphoresce smoke bombs to aid in assembling the group when the launching point was reached. Upon entering the assembly area, aircraft fire and enemy fighter opposition was encountered. Among the phosphoresce bombs launched by S/Sgt. Erwin, 1 proved faulty, exploding in the launching chute, and shot back into the interior of the aircraft, striking him in the face. The burning phosphoresce obliterated his nose and completely blinded him. Smoke filled the plane, obscuring the vision of the pilot. S/Sgt. Erwin realized that the aircraft and crew would be lost if the burning bomb remained in the plane.

Without regard for his own safety, he picked it up and feeling his way, instinctively, crawled around the gun turret and headed for the copilot's window. He found the navigator's table obstructing his passage. Grasping the burning bomb between his forearm and body, he unleashed the spring lock and raised the table. Struggling through the narrow passage he stumbled forward into the smoke-filled pilot's compartment. Groping with his burning hands, he located the window and threw the bomb out. Completely aflame, he fell back upon the floor. The smoke cleared, the pilot, at 300 feet, pulled the plane out of its dive.

S/Sgt. Erwin's gallantry and heroism above and beyond the call of duty saved the lives of his comrades.

Frederick E. Ferguson
U.S. Army • Vietnam

"When I speak to young men and women I try to always share the following poem:

It Has Always Been The Soldier
(author unknown)
It is the soldier, not the reporter
Who has given us freedom of the press;
It is the soldier, not the poet
Who has given us freedom of speech;
It is the soldier, not the campus organizer
Who has given us freedom to demonstrate;
It is the soldier
Who salutes the flag;
Who serves beneath the flag;
And whose coffin is draped by the flag.

"We are blessed to live in America. This is a nation where you can go as far as you want to go and you are able to go as far as your God-given talent will allow you to go. Stand up for what you believe, never compromise. Always do what is right, don't take the easy path, and never bow to peer pressure. Live by the code: Duty, honor, country."

Rank and organization
Chief Warrant Officer, U.S. Army, Company C, 227th Aviation
Battalion, 1st Cavalry Division (Airmobile).
Place and date
Hue, Republic of Vietnam, 31 January 1968.

CITATION

For conspicuous gallantry and intrepidity in action at the risk of his life above and beyond the call of duty. CWO Ferguson, U.S. Army distinguished himself while serving with Company C.

CWO Ferguson, commander of a resupply helicopter monitoring an emergency call from wounded passengers and crewmen of a downed helicopter under heavy attack within the enemy controlled city of Hue, unhesitatingly volunteered to attempt evacuation. Despite warnings from all aircraft to stay clear of the area due to heavy antiaircraft fire, CWO Ferguson began a low-level flight at maximum airspeed along the Perfume River toward the tiny, isolated South Vietnamese Army compound in which the crash survivors had taken refuge. Coolly and skillfully maintaining his course in the face of intense, short range fire from enemy occupied buildings and boats, he displayed superior flying skill and tenacity of purpose by landing his aircraft in an extremely confined area in a blinding dust cloud under heavy mortar and small-arms fire.

Although the helicopter was severely damaged by mortar fragments during the loading of the wounded, CWO Ferguson disregarded the damage and, taking off through the continuing hail of mortar fire, he flew his crippled aircraft on the return route through the rain of fire that he had experienced earlier and safely returned his wounded passengers to friendly control.

CWO Ferguson's extraordinary determination saved the lives of 5 of his comrades. His actions are in the highest traditions of the military service and reflect great credit on himself and the U.S. Army.

Lieutenant John W. Finn
U.S. Navy (Ret) • WWII

"The greatest thing about America and our people is their love of freedom, their love of nation, and patriotism. The Constitution, the Bill of Rights and our laws give us the right to worship and the right of free speech. If you don't have law, you will have anarchy. I have the greatest respect for our Founding Fathers. They gave us the right to be free. The reason so many people from all over the world want to come to America is because of our law, our Constitution, and the Bill of Rights.

"The advice that I want to stress to every young man and woman in America is: Always do what's right. Never give up. Be sure to continue your education. The one thing I regret most in my life is that I didn't pursue more education. Finally, love your nation and love freedom. They were purchased with a great cost."

Rank and organization
Lieutenant, U.S. Navy.
Place and date
Naval Air Station, Kaneohe Bay,
Territory of Hawaii, 7 December 1941.

CITATION

For extraordinary heroism distinguished service, and devotion above and beyond the call of duty.

During the first attack by Japanese airplanes on the Naval Air Station, Kaneohe Bay, on 7 December 1941, Lt. Finn promptly secured and manned a .50-caliber machinegun mounted on an instruction stand in a completely exposed section of the parking ramp, which was under heavy enemy machinegun strafing fire. Although painfully wounded many times, he continued to man this gun and to return the enemy's fire vigorously and with telling effect throughout the enemy strafing and bombing attacks and with complete disregard for his own personal safety.

It was only by specific orders that he was persuaded to leave his post to seek medical attention. Following first aid treatment, although obviously suffering much pain and moving with great difficulty, he returned to the squadron area and actively supervised the rearming of returning planes.

His extraordinary heroism and conduct in this action were in keeping with the highest traditions of the U.S. Naval Service.

Colonel Bernard F. Fisher
U.S. Air Force (Ret.) • Vietnam

"As a young man, prayer was always an important factor in my life. While in the Air Force, I had many opportunities to call on God for His help. The sheer terror of flying in weather, that at best many times was below minimums, gave me the privilege of calling for help. The day of the rescue, March 10, 1966, probably changed my life forever. I remember watching Jump Meyers' plane, flaming like a torch at the back past his tail after he was hit, and my telling him to dump his bombs and pull his gear up so he could belly it in. As I watched in horror, he skidded down the runway and off to the right. The plane burst into a huge ball of fire. I thought he was probably killed in the crash—then a gust of wind seemed to blow the flames from the right side and Jump came smoking out across the wing. It looked like he was burning as smoke and flames seemed to trail him. He jumped into a ditch at the side of the runway to hide from the enemy troops that were dangerously close.

"I called for a helicopter rescue, but they said it would be about 20 minutes. I went back to the battle with many thoughts racing through my mind. Going in to pick him up was not a good idea. However, I had such a strong feeling, so I decided to take a few minutes and seek counsel with my heavenly Father. I said, 'If this is what you want me to do, I need Your help. You have never let me down.' A calm peaceful feeling came over me, and I knew what I must do. My wingmen, John Lucas and Denny Hague, bless their hearts, said they would cover me. They were strafing right along the side of the runway, keeping the Vietnamese heads down. Denny said, 'If one of them had raised his head, we would've gotten him.'

"I will always be grateful for the 'Men in Blue' that I flew with and for those dedicated troops on the ground that kept the planes in tip-top condition and kept us flying. I will be eternally grateful for the help and protection I received that day from my heavenly Father!"

Rank and organization
Major, U.S. Air Force, 1st Air Commandos.
Place and date
Bien Hoa and Pleiku, Vietnam, 10 March 1966.

CITATION

For conspicuous gallantry and intrepidity at the risk of his life above and beyond the call of duty.

On that date, the special forces camp at A Shau was under attack by 2,000 North Vietnamese Army regulars. Hostile troops had positioned themselves between the airstrip and the camp. Other hostile troops had surrounded the camp and were continuously raking it with automatic weapons fire from the surrounding hills. The tops of the 1,500-foot hills were obscured by an 800-foot ceiling, limiting aircraft maneuverability and forcing pilots to operate within range of hostile gun positions, which often were able to fire down on the attacking aircraft.

During the battle, Maj. Fisher observed a fellow airman crash land on the battle-torn airstrip. In the belief that the downed pilot was seriously injured and in imminent danger of capture, Maj.

Fisher announced his intention to land on the airstrip to effect a rescue. Although aware of the extreme danger and likely failure of such an attempt, he elected to continue. Directing his own air cover, he landed his aircraft and taxied almost the full length of the runway, which was littered with battle debris and parts of an exploded aircraft. While effecting a successful rescue of the downed pilot, heavy ground fire was observed, with 19 bullets striking his aircraft. In the face of the withering ground fire, he applied power and gained enough speed to lift-off at the overrun of the airstrip.

Maj. Fisher's profound concern for his fellow airman, and at the risk of his life above and beyond the call of duty are in the highest traditions of the U.S. Air Force and reflect great credit upon himself and the Armed Forces of his country.

Conflicts Resulting
in MOH Awards

Civil War
Indian Wars 1861-1898
Korea 1871
Spanish American War
Philippines Samoa
Boxer Rebellion
Vera Cruz 1914
Haiti 1915
Dominican Republic
Haiti 1919-1920
Nicaragua 1927-1933
World War I
World War II
Korean War
Vietnam War
Somalia 1993

Michael J. Fitzmaurice
U.S. Army • Vietnam

"When asked about my creed or code of conduct for life, I had to do some serious thinking. I am a very quiet and private person. I have never felt comfortable expressing myself. But when passing on advice to the youth of America, I would tell them to stand up for what they believe in and be committed to their convictions and dreams. Never sell yourself short, give 100%, and it will come back to you a hundred fold. Always be honest, not only with the people around you, but mostly with yourself. Be kind to people, and grateful for the freedoms you share in this great nation because of the men and women who have served in the military.

"Our symbol of freedom in this country is the flag. I was once at a Memorial Day celebration where a tired, old soldier got up and read the words to the song 'Ragged Old Flag' by Johnny Cash. It told of the blood that was shed to keep 'Old Glory' flying. My wish is that whenever anyone sees Old Glory, they take one second and give thanks for this nation and the freedoms we enjoy."

Rank and organization
Specialist Fourth Class, U.S. Army, Troop D,
2d Squadron, 17th Cavalry, 101st Airborne Division.
Place and date
Khe Sanh, Republic of Vietnam, 23 March 1971.

CITATION

For conspicuous gallantry and intrepidity in action at the risk of his life above and beyond the call of duty. Sp4c. Fitzmaurice, 3d Platoon, Troop D, distinguished himself at Khe Sanh. Sp4c. Fitzmaurice and 3 fellow soldiers were occupying a bunker when a company of North Vietnamese sappers infiltrated the area. At the onset of the attack, Sp4c. Fitzmaurice observed 3 explosive charges which had been thrown into the bunker by the enemy. Realizing the imminent danger to his comrades, and with complete disregard for his personal safety, he hurled 2 of the charges out of the bunker. He then threw his flak vest and himself over the remaining charge. By this courageous act, he absorbed the blast and shielded his fellow-soldiers.

Although suffering from serious multiple wounds and partial loss of sight, he charged out of the bunker and engaged the enemy until his rifle was damaged by the blast of an enemy hand grenade. While in search of another weapon, Sp4c. Fitzmaurice encountered and overcame an enemy sapper in hand-to-hand combat. Having obtained another weapon, he returned to his original fighting position and inflicted additional casualties on the attacking enemy. Although seriously wounded, Sp4c. Fitzmaurice refused to be medically evacuated, preferring to remain at his post.

Sp4c. Fitzmaurice's extraordinary heroism in action at the risk of his life contributed significantly to the successful defense of the position and resulted in saving the lives of a number of his fellow soldiers. These acts of heroism go above and beyond the call of duty, are in keeping with the highest traditions of the military service, and reflect great credit on Sp4c. Fitzmaurice and the U.S. Army.

Rear Admiral Eugene B. Fluckey
U.S. Navy (Ret.) • WWII

"Serve your country well. Put more into life than you expect to get out of it. Drive yourself and lead others. Make others feel good about themselves and they will out-perform your expectations and you will never lack for friends. Count your blessings."

Rank and organization
Commander, U.S. Navy, Commanding U.S.S. Barb.
Place and date
Along coast of China, 19 December 1944 to 15 February 1945.
Other Navy award
Navy Cross with 3 Gold Stars.

CITATION

For conspicuous gallantry and intrepidity at the risk of his life above and beyond the call of duty as commanding officer of the U.S.S. Barb during her 11th war patrol along the east coast of China from 19 December 1944 to 15 February 1945.

After sinking a large enemy ammunition ship and damaging additional tonnage during a running 2-hour night battle on 8 January, Comdr. Fluckey, in an exceptional feat of brilliant deduction and bold tracking on 25 January, located a concentration of more than 30 enemy ships in the lower reaches of Nankuan Chiang (Mamkwan Harbor). Fully aware that a safe retirement would necessitate an hour's run at full speed through the uncharted, mined, and rock-obstructed waters, he bravely ordered, "Battle station—torpedoes!"

In a daring penetration of the heavy enemy screen, and riding in 5 fathoms of water, he launched the Barb's last forward torpedoes at 3,000-yard range. Quickly bringing the ship's stern tubes to bear, he turned loose 4 more torpedoes into the enemy, obtaining 8 direct hits on 6 of the main targets to explode a large ammunition ship and cause inestimable damage by the resultant flying shells and other pyrotechnics.

Clearing the treacherous area at high speed, he brought the Barb through to safety and 4 days later sank a large Japanese freighter to complete a record of heroic combat achievement, reflecting the highest credit upon Comdr. Fluckey, his gallant officers and men, and the U.S. Naval Service.

Lieutenant General Robert F. Foley
U.S. Army • Vietnam

"Life has its ups and downs as well as opportunities and adversity. Focusing on a desire to make a contribution to those around you provides not only a sense of gratification but a feeling of commitment and accomplishment. Self-worth comes from possessing the highest standards of integrity, consideration of others and faith in God. Those with strength of character will have the personal courage to carry out their moral obligation to respect, support, and provide for those who have been entrusted to their care."

Rank and organization
Captain, U.S. Army, Company A, 2d Battalion, 27th Infantry, 25th Infantry Division.
Place and date
Near Quan Dau Tieng, Republic of Vietnam, 5 November 1966.

CITATION
For conspicuous gallantry and intrepidity in action at the risk of his life above and beyond the call of duty. Capt. Foley's company was ordered to extricate another company of the battalion. Moving

through the dense jungle to aid the besieged unit, Company A encountered a strong enemy force occupying well concealed, defensive positions, and the company's leading element quickly sustained several casualties. Capt. Foley immediately ran forward to the scene of the most intense action to direct the company's efforts. Deploying 1 platoon on the flank, he led the other 2 platoons in an attack on the enemy in the face of intense fire. During this action, both radio operators accompanying him were wounded. At grave risk to himself, he defied the enemy's murderous fire and helped the wounded operators to a position where they could receive medical care.

As he moved forward again, 1 of his machine gun crews was wounded. Seizing the weapon, he charged forward firing the machine gun, shouting orders and rallying his men, thus maintaining the momentum of the attack. Under increasingly heavy enemy fire, he ordered his assistant to take cover and, alone, Capt. Foley continued to advance firing the machine gun until the wounded had been evacuated and the attack in this area could be resumed. When movement on the other flank was halted by the enemy's fanatical defense, Capt. Foley moved to personally direct this critical phase of the battle. Leading the renewed effort, he was blown off his feet and wounded by an enemy grenade.

Despite his painful wounds, he refused medical aid and persevered in the forefront of the attack on the enemy redoubt. He led the assault on several enemy gun emplacements and, single-handedly, destroyed 3 such positions. His outstanding personal leadership under intense enemy fire during the fierce battle, which lasted for several hours, inspired his men to heroic efforts and was instrumental in the ultimate success of the operation.

Capt. Foley's magnificent courage, selfless concern for his men and professional skill reflect the utmost credit upon himself and the U.S. Army.

Brigadier General Joseph Foss
U.S. Marine Corps, U.S. Air Force Reserve
(Ret.) USMC • WWII

"During World War II, God saved me over and over and over again. I have no excuse for being here. I often say that God was saving me for later duty. Bible study and sharing my faith occupy much of my time. I frequently speak to different groups and am often asked the question, 'Of all the honors and awards that you have received, what do you consider the most important, number one?' I am able to look them in the eye and say, 'The day that I invited Jesus Christ into my life as my Lord and Savior is number one.'"

Rank and organization
Captain, U.S. Marine Corps Reserve,
Marine Fighting Squadron 121, 1st Marine Aircraft Wing.
Place and date
Over Guadalcanal, 9 October to 19 November 1942,
15 and 23 January 1943.

CITATION

For outstanding heroism and courage above and beyond the call of duty as executive officer of Marine Fighting Squadron 121, 1st Marine Aircraft Wing, at Guadalcanal. Engaging in almost daily combat with the enemy from 9 October to 19 November 1942, Capt. Foss personally shot down 23 Japanese planes and damaged others so severely that their destruction was extremely probable.

In addition, during this period, he successfully led a large number of escort missions, skillfully covering reconnaissance, bombing, and photographic planes as well as surface craft. On 15 January 1943, he added 3 more enemy planes to his already brilliant successes for a record of aerial combat achievement unsurpassed in this war. Boldly searching out an approaching enemy force on 25 January, Capt. Foss led his 8 F-4F Marine planes and 4 Army P-38s into action and, undaunted by tremendously superior numbers, intercepted and struck with such force that 4 Japanese fighters were shot down and the bombers were turned back without releasing a single bomb.

His remarkable flying skill, inspiring leadership, and indomitable fighting spirit were distinctive factors in the defense of strategic American positions on Guadalcanal.

SAVED FOR LATER DUTY

It was November of 1943 and I was about to experience one of the most frightening experiences of my life. While on a mission, we spotted a Japanese flotilla with air cover from six float Zeros, equipped with pontoons for water takeoffs. We were able to shoot down the six Zeros but not without the loss of one of our planes and pilot.

As we prepared to attack the Japanese ships, I spotted another Japanese plane. I flew upward to get above the bogey. When he emerged from the cloud, I made a diving run toward the plane. I quickly realized that I had overestimated my adversary. The plane was not the faster and nimbler Zero but was a slower scout plane with a rear gunner. I dove too fast and had to roll on my side to avoid crashing into the rear of the plane. The pilot rolled as well, giving his tail gunner a perfect shot at me, at point blank range. The shells pierced the left side of my engine cowling and shattered the canopy of the side of my plane just a few inches from my face. Initially it appeared that there was no serious damage, but because of the damage to my plane, I was unable to dive and I watched the planes of VMF-121 attack the Japanese ships. With a second pass, I was able to shoot down the scout plane and then came upon a second scout plane that I was also able to bring down—my eighteenth and nineteenth victory in air combat.

As I looked for the rest of my flight, I saw them off in the distance over a mile away flying to get out of range of the ship's gun to regroup and head back to the base. I tried to call the departing planes but couldn't raise anyone. Apparently the radio was dead, probably one of the Japanese shells had damaged the aerial. As the engine of the plane started to miss and backfire puffing out white smoke, I headed for the rendezvous point. I had to throttle back repeatedly to prevent the engine from conking out. At this point I was getting nervous. The others had long since regrouped and headed back. I was beginning to lose altitude when I ran into rain-squalls and heavy clouds.

Breaking out of the clouds, I could make out two islands and I headed toward them. I mistook them for the gateway to Guadalcanal. After awhile the engine stops got closer than the starts, and I realized that I wasn't going to make it back to Henderson Field. Another squall appeared dead ahead and I flew to circumvent it. When I came abreast of the storm, the engine stopped cold. I knew that if I landed in the water, my chances of being spotted were minimal, if not nonexistent. I lamented the fact that I had never learned to swim. I spotted an island and I set my glide path for it. I figured that I had plenty of altitude to make the distance. I planned to ditch the plane directly offshore and paddle to land with the aid of my Mae West. Believing that I might find a sandy beach to land on, I circled over the deserted shoreline. I realized that I miscalculated: The maneuver cost me the needed altitude.

When I circled back out to sea I realized that I was going down in the water about five miles from land. As the plane descended and the water rose to meet me, I pulled the nose of the plane up, hoping to skip the plane along the surface of the water. The tail hit the water and bounced up above the front of the plane. When I hit the water a second time, I nosed into the Pacific like a torpedo from a dive-bomber. The heavily armored plane sank almost immediately. I found myself in utter darkness with water gushing into the cockpit. Trapped in the plane, I forced myself to act. As water filled the cockpit, I felt for the latches that held the canopy, unfastened them, and pushed it open with all my strength. I fought to maintain consciousness, but momentarily blacked out and sucked in the brackish sea water. Just as the story goes, my whole life passed before my eyes. Forcing myself to action was agony, and I restrained my gagging through sheer force of will. Reaching down I unhooked my leg straps, swallowing more sea water in the process.

No longer locked in the plane, I was pulled upward toward the surface by the force of the current streaming past the rapidly sinking Wildcat. At the same time my left foot caught and wedged under the cockpit seat, trapping me and holding me fast as the Wildcat continued its descent into the deep. I pulled my way, hand over hand, toward my captured foot. I used the last of my strength to free myself and I felt the crushing pressure of the cold water as I shot upward. My need for air was pure pain. When I hit the surface I adjusted the straps of my Mae West and all of a sudden I was floating.

I realized the odds of making it to the island were slim, between the storm, the rapidly approaching darkness, and the current that seemed to be carrying me out to sea. To make matters worse, a short distance away something caught my eye, "Shark fins!" I believe I even yelled it out loud! I thought, "What a way to go. After all I've been through, I'm going to check out as a hunk of shark bait." Trying to swim became doubly fearful. Every time I reached an arm out to paddle I was afraid I'd draw back a stub. I started praying harder than I'd ever prayed in my life. I confessed every sin I could remember and kept praying, "God help me." I never felt more alone or helpless. I drifted for four or five hours. I was growing weaker as I struggled against the sea. Through the black of the night I heard something. Voices! I turned my head in the direction of the sounds. Canoe paddles? "Japs," I thought! "They saw me go down." I stopped swimming and floated silently. The splashing of the oars grew louder. Two boats were traveling toward me, I heard men speaking but could not make out the mumbled conversations. The searchers combed the waters, back and forth. Finally someone yelled, "Lets look over 'ere." It was an Australian accent, and the most welcome sound I'd ever heard. "Hey!" I yelled. "Over here!" A hand reached out of the darkness and pulled me into the outrigger. It was the hand of Father Dan Stuyvenberg, a Catholic priest. As the men talked they told me that the piece of land that I'd been swimming toward was populated with man-eating crocodiles.

Today I realize that God saved me over and over and over. I have no excuse for being in the world today except that the Lord was saving me for another battle. I could have been killed by the gunfire that brought my plane down. I could have died in the crash landing, could have drowned, could have been killed by sharks or man-eating crocodiles or captured and killed by the Japanese, but God saved me.

Adapted from *A PROUD AMERICAN, The Autobiography of Joe Foss*, Pocket Books.

The National Headquarters and Museum for the Congressional MOH

Located on the hangar deck of the USS Yorktown at Patriots Point, this museum details the eight eras of Medal of Honor history: The Civil War; Indian Campaigns; Wars of American Expansion; Peacetime; World War I; World War II; Korea; and Vietnam. The panels list all of the Medal of Honor recipients to date and include such well-known names as Audie Murphy, Sergeant Alvin York, and Jimmie Doolittle.

Exhibits include memorabilia and artifacts relating to Medal of Honor recipients and archives of important documents. In addition to the permanent exhibit, rotating displays focus on related areas of interest.

The National Headquarters and Museum for the Congressional Medal of Honor is located at 40 Patriots Point Road, Mt. Pleasant, SC 29464, aboard the aircraft carrier USS Yorktown, the centerpiece of Patriots Point Naval and Maritime Museum.

Colonel Wesley L. Fox
U.S. Marine Corps (Ret.) • Vietnam

"Leadership is causing others to reach deep down inside themselves and pull up that quality that they never knew they possessed. Leadership is very important in our society today; it is needed in all occupations and lifestyles. Some men and women are born with a natural leadership ability and have taken charge and shown the way all their lives. I believe good leadership can also be learned, practiced, and exercised. Where does one go to learn how to lead others, to receive a degree in something as important as inspiring others to follow? Except for the military services, there are not many institutions offering this field of study.

"Learning leadership includes knowing what others expect and like to see in their leader: someone who cares about them, communicates with them, and sets a good example. Good leaders must also be good followers. Those who want to lead others must learn what is required of an individual in performing that important task. Correctness of self and unquestionable integrity are the foundation blocks. Other traits include knowledge, dependability, and decisiveness, but overshadowing these and other traits is courage. Without courage in its many forms, the other traits pale and fall short in their own right."

"Good character, principles, and ethical standards are needed and are very important to a leader. Today, personal interest conflicts hound many important leaders within our society either because they did not study the art of leadership or did not consider the consequences of personality flaws while they violated good leadership principles. These are unfortunate circumstances since everyone loses under a leader who operates out of a weakened position. Leaders must remain above the cannon of personality infliction. A man's word is his bond that holds him accountable. There is no gray area within the meaning of integrity—you did, or you did not; you will or you will not. Period!"

———

Rank and organization
Captain, U.S. Marine Corps, Company A,
1st Battalion, 9th Marines, 3d Marine Division.
Place and date
Quang Tri Province, Republic of Vietnam, 22 February 1969.

CITATION
For conspicuous gallantry and intrepidity at the risk of his life above and beyond the call of duty while serving as commanding officer of Company A, in action against the enemy in the northern A Shau Valley.

Capt. (then 1st Lt.) Fox's company came under intense fire from a large well concealed enemy force. Capt. Fox maneuvered to a position from which he could assess the situation and confer with his platoon leaders. As they departed to execute the plan he had devised, the enemy attacked and Capt. Fox was wounded along with all of the other members of the command group, except the executive officer. Capt. Fox continued to direct the activity of his company. Advancing through heavy enemy fire, he personally neutralized 1 enemy position and calmly ordered an assault against the hostile emplacements. He then moved through the hazardous area coordinating aircraft support with the activities of his men.

When his executive officer was mortally wounded, Capt. Fox reorganized the company and directed the fire of his men as they hurled grenades against the enemy and drove the hostile forces into retreat. Wounded again in the final assault, Capt. Fox refused medical attention, established a defensive posture, and supervised the preparation of casualties for medical evacuation. His indomitable courage, inspiring initiative, and unwavering devotion to duty in the face of grave personal danger inspired his marines to such aggressive action that they overcame all enemy resistance and destroyed a large bunker complex.

Capt. Fox's heroic actions reflect great credit upon himself and the Marine Corps, and uphold the highest traditions of the U.S. Naval Service.

Who Are They?

The first award of the Medal of Honor was made March 25, 1863 to Private Jacob Parrott and five others. There have been:

3,459 Medals of Honor awarded

For 3,454 separate acts of heroism

Performed by 3,440 individuals
(including 9 "Unknown Soldiers")

As of Jan. 7, 2003 there are 139 Living Recipients

Surviving Recipients by conflict:

World War II - 53
Korea - 20
Vietnam - 66

Nineteen of these were awarded as a second award to men who had already received a previous Medal of Honor. Five of the 19 double awardees were Marines who, during World War I worked closely with members of the Army and were awarded both the Army and Navy Medals of Honor for the same action. The other 14 double awardees received their second Medal of Honor for a second heroic action.

The last action in which the Medal of Honor was awarded was Mogadishu, Somalia on October 3, 1993. The Medals were awarded posthumously to the families of Gary I. Gordon and Randall D. Shugart, who were members of "The Delta Force" aka Special Forces Operational Detachment Delta.

Major Edward W. Freeman
U.S. Army (Ret.) • Vietnam

"When I was a young boy, my father sold some cattle to a farmer. The man only had half the money to buy the cattle. I remember my father shaking the farmer's hand after he loaded the cattle. When I asked my father why the man was leaving with the cattle but had only paid half of the money, my dad responded, 'Don't worry. He is an honest man.' A few weeks later the farmer returned with the remainder of the money. That incident taught me a great lesson.

"Many years later I purchased some railroad ties to complete a project. They cost ninety-eight cents apiece. When I finished the project, I had too many railroad ties left over. I told a man that I would sell the ties for what I paid for them. Another man was also interested in the ties and asked if I would sell them to him. When I told him I had already promised them to another man, he offered to give me more money if I would sell them to him. I explained that I couldn't sell them to him because my honor wasn't for sale.

"I learned this from my father and I would offer it as my advice for life. Always be honest; your word is your bond. Moral courage is important; doing what's right is as important as physical courage. Finally, we need to remember, put God first, then country and both before self!"

CITATION

Captain Ed W. Freeman, United States Army, distinguished himself by numerous acts of conspicuous gallantry and extraordinary intrepidity on 14 November 1965 while serving with Company A, 229th Assault Helicopter Battalion, 1st Cavalry Division (Airmobile).

As a flight leader and second in command of a 16-helicopter lift unit, he supported a heavily engaged American infantry battalion at Landing Zone X-Ray in the Ia Drang Valley, Republic of Vietnam. The unit was almost out of ammunition after taking some of the heaviest casualties of the war, fighting off a relentless attack from a highly motivated, heavily armed enemy force. When the infantry commander closed the helicopter landing zone due to intense direct enemy fire, Captain Freeman risked his own life by flying his unarmed helicopter through a gauntlet of enemy fire time after time, delivering critically needed ammunition, water and medical supplies to the besieged battalion. His flights had a direct impact on the battle's outcome by providing the engaged units with timely supplies of ammunition critical to their survival, without which they would almost surely have gone down, with much greater loss of life.

After medical evacuation helicopters refused to fly into the area due to intense enemy fire, Captain Freeman flew 14 separate rescue missions, providing life-saving evacuation of an estimated 30 seriously wounded soldiers—some of whom would not have survived had he not acted. All flights were made into a small emergency landing zone within 100 to 200 meters of the defensive perimeter where heavily committed units were perilously holding off the attacking elements. Captain Freeman's selfless acts of great valor, extraordinary perseverance, and intrepidity were far above and beyond the call of duty or mission and set a superb example of leadership and courage for all of his peers.

Captain Freeman's extraordinary heroism and devotion to duty are in keeping with the highest traditions of military service and reflect great credit upon himself, his unit, and the United States Army.

Lieutenant Colonel Harold A. Fritz
U.S. Army (Ret.) • Vietnam

"My Creed or Code of Conduct remains rather simplistic:
1. Lead by example.
2. Don't expect the impossible—but maintain the highest of standards.
3. Always protect and stand up for your subordinates— that is an important part of a leader's responsibility.
4. When the odds against you are at an all time high— daring maneuvers and preciseness of execution will be your ingredients for success.
5. Whatever your religious convictions may be—always maintain faith!"

Rank and organization
Captain, U.S. Army, Troop A, 1st Squadron, 11th Armored Cavalry Regiment.
Place and date
Binh Long Province, Republic of Vietnam, 11 January 1969.

CITATION
For conspicuous gallantry and intrepidity in action at the risk of

his life above and beyond the call of duty. Capt. (then 1st Lt.) Fritz, Armor, U.S. Army, distinguished himself while serving as a platoon leader with Troop A, near Quan Loi.

Capt. Fritz was leading his 7-vehicle armored column along Highway 13 to meet and escort a truck convoy when the column suddenly came under intense crossfire from a reinforced enemy company deployed in ambush positions. In the initial attack, Capt. Fritz' vehicle was hit and he was seriously wounded. Realizing that his platoon was completely surrounded, vastly outnumbered, and in danger of being overrun, Capt. Fritz leaped to the top of his burning vehicle and directed the positioning of his remaining vehicles and men. With complete disregard for his wounds and safety, he ran from vehicle to vehicle in complete view of the enemy gunners in order to reposition his men, to improve the defenses, to assist the wounded, to distribute ammunition, to direct fire, and to provide encouragement to his men.

When a strong enemy force assaulted the position and attempted to overrun the platoon, Capt. Fritz manned a machine gun, and through his exemplary action, inspired his men to deliver intense and deadly fire which broke the assault and routed the attackers. Moments later a second enemy force advanced to within 2 meters of the position and threatened to overwhelm the defenders. Capt. Fritz, armed only with a pistol and bayonet, led a small group of his men in a fierce and daring charge which routed the attackers and inflicted heavy casualties.

When a relief force arrived, Capt. Fritz saw that it was not deploying effectively against the enemy positions, and he moved through the heavy enemy fire to direct its deployment against the hostile positions. This deployment forced the enemy to abandon the ambush site and withdraw. Despite his wounds, Capt. Fritz returned to his position, assisted his men, and refused medical attention until all of his wounded comrades had been treated and evacuated.

The extraordinary courage and selflessness displayed by Capt. Fritz, at the repeated risk of his own life above and beyond the call of duty, were in keeping with the highest traditions of the U.S. Army and reflect the greatest credit upon himself, his unit, and the Armed Forces.

Brigadier General Robert E. Galer
U.S. Marine Corps (Ret.) • WWII

"Just realize that the Lord is always with you. Know that if you have 'good luck' or 'bad luck,' He is well aware and probably responsible for your good luck.

"Set your goals where you want to go in life, usually the top, then go for it. Don't let anything stop you from striving for the goal you have set, and the Lord will be with you. Always remember: Keep your word. If you make a commitment, then do it. Honesty is the best policy.

"I claim to be the luckiest Marine alive. Thanks to our Lord, I survived five aircraft crashes (shot down four times). My son says, 'Pop, you're an enemy Ace.' I believe the Lord was with me. *Semper Fi.*"

Rank and organization
Major, U.S. Marine Corps, Marine Fighter Sqdn. 244.
Place
Solomon Islands Area.
Other Navy awards
Navy Cross, Distinguished Flying Cross.

CITATION

For conspicuous heroism and courage above and beyond the call of duty as leader of a marine fighter squadron in aerial combat with enemy Japanese forces in the Solomon Islands area.

Leading his squadron repeatedly in daring and aggressive raids against Japanese aerial forces, vastly superior in numbers, Maj. Galer availed himself of every favorable attack opportunity, individually shooting down 11 enemy bomber and fighter aircraft over a period of 29 days. Though suffering the extreme physical strain attendant upon protracted fighter operations at an altitude above 25,000 feet, the squadron under his zealous and inspiring leadership shot down a total of 27 Japanese planes.

His superb airmanship, his outstanding skill and personal valor reflect great credit upon Maj. Galer's gallant fighting spirit and upon the U.S. Naval Service.

Nathan G. Gordon
U.S. Navy • WWII

"As the grandson of a Methodist minister, I heard about the importance of faith in God and the Golden Rule at an early age. My advice for life, my creed, is to live by the Golden Rule: Always do unto others as you would have them do unto you."

Rank and organization
Lieutenant, U.S. Navy, commander of Catalina patrol plane.
Place and date
Bismarck Sea, 15 February 1944.

CITATION

For extraordinary heroism above and beyond the call of duty as commander of a Catalina patrol plane in rescuing personnel of the U.S. Army 5th Air Force shot down in combat over Kavieng Harbor in the Bismarck Sea, 15 February 1944.

On air alert in the vicinity of Vitu Islands, Lt. (then Lt. j.g.) Gordon unhesitatingly responded to a report of the crash and flew boldly into the harbor, defying close-range fire from enemy shore guns to make 3 separate landings in full view of the Japanese and pick up 9 men, several of them injured. With his cumbersome flying boat dangerously overloaded, he made a brilliant takeoff despite heavy swells and almost total absence of wind and set a course for base, only to receive the report of another group stranded in a rubber life raft 600 yards from the enemy shore.

Promptly turning back, he again risked his life to set his plane down under direct fire of the heaviest defenses of Kavieng and take aboard 6 more survivors, coolly making his fourth dexterous takeoff with 15 rescued officers and men.

By his exceptional daring, personal valor, and incomparable airmanship under most perilous conditions, Lt. Gordon prevented certain death or capture of our airmen by the Japanese.

Stephen R. Gregg
U.S. Army • WWII

"As a young boy I used to get down on my knees every night with my mother at my side to pray. When I finished my prayers, I would climb into bed and my mother would leave the room. She often found me later kneeling at the bedside once again. When she asked why I wasn't asleep and in bed, I would explain that I remembered something else I needed to pray about.

"I want you to know it is very difficult for an 88-year-old man to get down on his knees to pray, but I still do so every night. I still remember all those men who served and gave their lives for our nation. It's important to pray.

"If you are going to do something, then do it right. I believe my basic Ranger training helped to save me because it taught me how to go into battle, to not get excited, and to do the right thing, the way it had to be done.

"During the invasion of Salerno, Italy, we were surrounded. We received horrible incoming fire from every angle. Most of the men in my unit were captured, wounded, or killed. Of the 198 men, only 27 survived. I was able to lead seven of those men to safety.

"I would encourage you to always do the right thing. Work hard, be persistent, and have a positive attitude."

Rank and organization
Second Lieutenant, U.S. Army,
143d Infantry, 36th Infantry Division.
Place and date
Near Montelimar, France, 27 August 1944.

CITATION

For conspicuous gallantry and intrepidity at risk of life above and beyond the call of duty on 27 August 1944, in the vicinity of Montelimar, France.

As his platoon advanced upon the enemy positions, the leading scout was fired upon and 2d Lt. Gregg (then a Tech. Sgt.) immediately put his machineguns into action to cover the advance of the riflemen. The Germans, who were at close range, threw hand grenades at the riflemen, killing some and wounding 7. Each time a medical aid man attempted to reach the wounded, the Germans fired at him. Realizing the seriousness of the situation, 2d Lt. Gregg took 1 of the light .30-caliber machineguns, and firing from the hip, started boldly up the hill with the medical aid man following him. Although the enemy was throwing hand grenades at him, 2d Lt. Gregg remained and fired into the enemy positions while the medical aid man removed the 7 wounded men to safety.

When 2d Lt. Gregg had expended all his ammunition, he was covered by 4 Germans who ordered him to surrender. Since the attention of most of the Germans had been diverted by watching this action, friendly riflemen were able to maneuver into firing positions. One, seeing 2d Lt. Gregg's situation, opened fire on his captors. The 4 Germans hit the ground and thereupon 2d Lt. Gregg recovered a machine pistol from one of the Germans and managed to escape to his other machinegun positions. He manned a gun, firing at his captors, killed 1 of them and wounded the other. This action so discouraged the Germans that the platoon was able to continue its advance up the hill to achieve its objective.

The following morning, just prior to daybreak, the Germans launched a strong attack, supported by tanks, in an attempt to drive

Company L from the hill. As these tanks moved along the valley and their foot troops advanced up the hill, 2d Lt. Gregg immediately ordered his mortars into action.

During the day, by careful observation, he was able to direct effective fire on the enemy, inflicting heavy casualties. By late afternoon he had directed 600 rounds when his communication to the mortars was knocked out. Without hesitation, he started checking his wires, although the area was under heavy enemy small arms and artillery fire. When he was within 100 yards of his mortar position, 1 of his men informed him that the section had been captured and the Germans were using the mortars to fire on the company. 2d Lt. Gregg with this man and another nearby rifleman started for the gun position where he could see 5 Germans firing his mortars. He ordered the 2 men to cover him, crawled up, threw a hand grenade into the position, and then charged it. The hand grenade killed 1, injured 2, 2d Lt. Gregg took the other 2 prisoners, and put his mortars back into action.

MOH WAS AWARDED
TO 9 UNKNOWN SOLDIERS

ONE UNKNOWN WWI SOLDIER EACH
FROM THE COUNTRIES OF:

BELGIUM

GREAT BRITAIN

FRANCE

ITALY

RUMANIA

AND ONE UNKNOWN AMERICAN
WHO GAVE HIS LIFE DURING EACH
OF THE FOLLOWING CONFLICTS:

WWI

WWII

KOREA

VIETNAM

Lieutenant Colonel Charles Hagemeister
U.S. Army (Ret.) • Vietnam

"I have a coin that I sometimes carry in my pocket. The coin has the words 'American Liberties' on it. One side of the coin has the word 'rights' and the other side has the word 'responsibilities.' One important responsibility is to obtain your voter registration card as soon as you are old enough to do so and then exercise the right to vote. If you don't vote, then you don't have the right to complain about how things are going.

"As far as values and the teaching of values, we must teach our children the values we believe in and hold dear. I would also like to stress the importance of character and integrity in life. Integrity is doing what is right when no one is watching. I would also encourage you to stand up for what you believe in and have faith in God."

Rank and organization
Specialist Fifth Class (then Sp4c.) U.S. Army, Headquarters and Headquarters Company, 1st Battalion, 5th Cavalry, 1st Cavalry Division (Airmobile).
Place and date
Binh Dinh Province, Republic of Vietnam, 20 March 1967.

CITATION

For conspicuous gallantry and intrepidity in action at the risk of his life above and beyond the call of duty.

While conducting combat operations against a hostile force, Sp5c. Hagemeister's platoon suddenly came under heavy attack from 3 sides by an enemy force occupying well-concealed, fortified positions and supported by machine guns and mortars. Seeing 2 of his comrades seriously wounded in the initial action, Sp5c. Hagemeister unhesitatingly and with total disregard for his safety, raced through the deadly hail of enemy fire to provide them medical aid. Upon learning that the platoon leader and several other soldiers also had been wounded, Sp5c. Hagemeister continued to brave the withering enemy fire and crawled forward to render lifesaving treatment and to offer words of encouragement.

Attempting to evacuate the seriously wounded soldiers, Sp5c. Hagemeister was taken under fire at close range by an enemy sniper. Realizing that the lives of his fellow soldiers depended on his actions, Sp5c. Hagemeister seized a rifle from a fallen comrade, killed the sniper and 3 other enemy soldiers who were attempting to encircle his position, and silenced an enemy machine gun that covered the area with deadly fire. Unable to remove the wounded to a less exposed location and aware of the enemy's efforts to isolate his unit, he dashed through the fusillade of fire to secure help from a nearby platoon. Returning with help, he placed men in positions to cover his advance as he moved to evacuate the wounded forward of his location.

These efforts successfully completed, he then moved to the other flank and evacuated additional wounded men despite the fact that his every move drew fire from the enemy. Sp5c. Hagemeister's repeated heroic and selfless actions at the risk of his life saved the lives of many of his comrades and inspired their actions in repelling the enemy assault. Sp5c. Hagemeister's indomitable courage was in the highest traditions of the U.S. Armed Forces and reflect great credit upon himself.

John D. Hawk
U.S. Army • WWII

"Whatever you do in life, give it your best effort. If you are honest with yourself and can truthfully say you gave it your best effort—it has to be acceptable. Anyone who cannot accept or understand this is not worth much attention."

Rank and organization
Sergeant, U.S. Army, Company E,
359th Infantry, 90th Infantry Division.
Place and date
Near Chambois, France, 20 August 1944.

CITATION

He manned a light machinegun on 20 August 1944, near Chambois, France, a key point in the encirclement which created the Falaise Pocket. During an enemy counterattack, his position was menaced by a strong force of tanks and infantry. His fire forced the infantry to withdraw, but an artillery shell knocked out his gun and wounded him in the right thigh. Securing a bazooka, he and another man stalked the tanks and forced them to retire to a wooded section. In the lull which followed, Sgt. Hawk reorganized 2 machinegun squads and, in the face of intense enemy fire, directed the assembly of 1 workable weapon from 2 damaged guns.

When another enemy assault developed, he was forced to pull back from the pressure of spearheading armor. Two of our tank destroyers were brought up. Their shots were ineffective because of the terrain until Sgt. Hawk, despite his wound, boldly climbed to an exposed position on a knoll where, unmoved by fusillades from the enemy, he became a human aiming stake for the destroyers. Realizing that his shouted fire directions could not be heard above the noise of battle, he ran back to the destroyers through a concentration of bullets and shrapnel to correct the range. He returned to his exposed position, repeating this performance until 2 of the tanks were knocked out and a third driven off. Still at great risk, he continued to direct the destroyers' fire into the Germans' wooded position until the enemy came out and surrendered.

Sgt. Hawk's fearless initiative and heroic conduct, even while suffering from a painful wound, was in large measure responsible for crushing 2 desperate attempts of the enemy to escape from the Falaise Picket and for taking more than 500 prisoners.

Shizuya Hayashi
U.S. Army • WWII

"The advice my parents gave to me as a boy and as a young man was: Do your best, do what you know is right, never give up, always be honest, and work hard.

"I would also offer this advice: when something needs to be done—do it. Don't wait for someone else to do it. I also believe you should never ask someone to do something that you are unwilling to do yourself.

"As a soldier in the Army, I was told to obey orders and respect authority. I also learned about the importance of honor.

"Finally, I would encourage everyone to live by the Golden Rule: Do unto others as you would have them do unto you."

CITATION

Private Shizuya Hayashi distinguished himself by extraordinary heroism in action on 29 November 1943, near Cerasuolo, Italy.

During a flank assault on high ground held by the enemy, Private Hayashi rose alone in the face of grenade, rifle, and machine gun fire. Firing his automatic rifle from the hip, he charged and overtook an enemy machine gun position, killing seven men in the nest and two more as they fled.

After his platoon advanced 200 yards from this point, an enemy antiaircraft gun opened fire on the men. Private Hayashi returned fire at the hostile position, killing nine of the enemy, taking four prisoners, and forcing the remainder of the force to withdraw from the hill.

Private Hayashi's extraordinary heroism and devotion to duty are in keeping with the highest traditions of military service and reflect great credit on him, his unit, and the United States Army.

Master Sergeant James R. Hendrix
U.S. Army (Ret.) • WWII

"I grew up on a farm near Lapanto, Arkansas. As one of ten kids in the family I decided to leave school early to work on the farm. During WWII, I joined the service and served in the Army for twenty-two years. The Army made it possible for me to complete my high school education on active duty. Some of the advice that I would offer is to make every effort to complete your education.

"In life you will face difficulties but never give up, even when life is tough. As a soldier I realized that it is important to never ask someone to do something that you are not willing to do yourself.

"Over the years I have learned how important it is to trust in God and to live by the Golden Rule. Finally, I want to encourage every young man and women to love and serve God."

Rank and organization
Private, U.S. Army, Company C,
53d Armored Infantry Battalion, 4th Armored Division.
Place and date
Near Assenois, Belgium, 26 December 1944.

CITATION

On the night of 26 December 1944, near Assenois, Belgium, he was with the leading element engaged in the final thrust to break through to the besieged garrison at Bastogne when halted by a fierce combination of artillery and small arms fire. He dismounted from his half-track and advanced against two 88mm. guns, and, by the ferocity of his rifle fire, compelled the guncrews to take cover and then to surrender.

Later in the attack he again left his vehicle, voluntarily, to aid 2 wounded soldiers, helpless and exposed to intense machinegun fire. Effectively silencing 2 hostile machineguns, he held off the enemy by his own fire until the wounded men were evacuated. Pvt. Hendrix again distinguished himself when he hastened to the aid of still another soldier who was trapped in a burning half-track. Braving enemy sniper fire and exploding mines and ammunition in the vehicle, he extricated the wounded man and extinguished his flaming clothing, thereby saving the life of his fellow soldier.

Pvt. Hendrix, by his superb courage and heroism, exemplified the highest traditions of the military service.

Rodolfo "Rudy" Hernandez
U.S. Army • Korea

"I believe in God Almighty. There were times in my life that God meant more to me than anyone else. He forgives us of sin, gives us abundant life, and is full of mercy.

"I was pleased to fight for my country not only because I was born in the United States, but because I believe it is the land of promise and hope.

"Finally, I love the flag. I hold it in respect."

Rank and organization
Corporal, U.S. Army, Company G,
187th Airborne Regimental Combat Team.
Place and date
Near Wontong-ni, Korea, 31 May 1951.

CITATION

Cpl. Hernandez, a member of Company G, distinguished himself by conspicuous gallantry and intrepidity above and beyond the call of duty in action against the enemy.

His platoon, in defensive positions on Hill 420, came under ruthless attack by a numerically superior and fanatical hostile force, accompanied by heavy artillery, mortar, and machine gun fire which inflicted numerous casualties on the platoon. His comrades were forced to withdraw due to lack of ammunition but Cpl. Hernandez, although wounded in an exchange of grenades, continued to deliver deadly fire into the ranks of the onrushing assailants until a ruptured cartridge rendered his rifle inoperative. Immediately leaving his position, Cpl. Hernandez rushed the enemy armed only with rifle and bayonet. Fearlessly engaging the foe, he killed 6 of the enemy before falling unconscious from grenade, bayonet, and bullet wounds but his heroic action momentarily halted the enemy advance and enabled his unit to counterattack and retake the lost ground.

The indomitable fighting spirit, outstanding courage, and tenacious devotion to duty clearly demonstrated by Cpl. Hernandez reflect the highest credit upon himself, the infantry, and the U.S. Army.

I AM NOT ASHAMED

I am proud to be a Medal of Honor recipient. I am also proud of my Hispanic heritage, of being an American, and of being an Army paratrooper. I carry a business card with the image of the Medal of Honor and my name on the front of the card. When you turn the card over, you will read the words, "I am not ashamed of the gospel of Jesus Christ." Faith in God is an important part of my life. I have a deep faith in God because He has been so good to me.

During the Korean War, I was an Army Infantryman with the 187th Regimental Combat Team, frequently referred to as the RAAKASANS. I was already an experienced combat veteran by February 1951. During one battle I changed places with my friend, and he was killed almost immediately. I realized that bullet was meant for me.

On the 31st of May, 1951, my platoon came under a ruthless attack by a numerically superior enemy force. We were near Wontong-ni, Korea on Hill 420. The initial attack was from heavy artillery, mortar, and machine-gun fire and was followed by an overwhelming number of enemy soldiers.

Many of the men in the platoon were wounded and the decision was made to withdraw. I remained to cover the withdrawal even though I was wounded by artillery shrapnel. While I was firing my rifle, one of the cartridges in my weapon ruptured and rendered the rifle inoperable. I placed the bayonet on my rifle and rushed toward the enemy. I made the decision to counter-attack in an effort to save the lives of my comrades.

During the counter-attack, I was severely wounded by artillery shrapnel from an air-burst and rifle fire, and I was bayoneted twice. But my efforts halted their assault, which allowed my unit to counterattack and retake our position. I was wounded so severely that I was placed in a body bag because everyone assumed that I was dead. Someone finally realized that I was still alive when they saw my hand move.

The artillery shrapnel tore my helmet from my head and a large part of my skull and a part of my brain was severely injured. I was paralyzed, unconscious, and in a coma for a month. When I finally regained consciousness, I had to learn how to swallow, eat, feed myself, walk, and speak. I was transferred to Letterman Army Hospital in San Francisco where surgeons tried to repair the damage to my skull, face, arm, and leg. A large part of my skull had been destroyed and the surgeons performed experimental surgery to close the large defect in my skull. Months passed before I was able to speak a single word.

It took twelve years for me to recover from the massive injuries that I sustained. I underwent multiple surgeries for five years and spent the next eight years working to regain control of my body. I still do not have complete use of my right arm and hand, but I learned to write and do most things with my left hand.

After all I have been through, I came to the conclusion that only by the grace of God and His mercy am I alive today. It gives me great joy to be able to say and to share with others that "I am not ashamed of the gospel of Jesus Christ."

—*Rodolfo "Rudy" Hernandez*

Colonel Robert L. Howard
U.S. Army (Ret.) • Vietnam

"A soldier knows that he is a part of an essential organization. His mission and his manner of performance help to guarantee the safety and security of our country. The moral basis for a soldier's behavior is his philosophy of life, which is the product of his family upbringing, education, religious training, and life experience, including his life in the Army. Because he believes in morality, he tries at all times to act according to that belief. A soldier cannot be truly loyal to his superiors unless he is loyal to his subordinates and peers. To be an effective link in the chain of command, he must extend his ties of loyalty to all members of the unit."

Rank and organization
First Lieutenant, U.S. Army, 5th Special Forces
Group (Airborne), 1st Special Forces.
Place and date
Republic of Vietnam, 30 December 1968.

CITATION
For conspicuous gallantry and intrepidity in action at the risk of

his life above and beyond the call of duty. 1st Lt. Howard (then Sfc.), distinguished himself while serving as platoon sergeant of an American-Vietnamese platoon which was on a mission to rescue a missing American soldier in enemy controlled territory in the Republic of Vietnam.

The platoon had left its helicopter landing zone and was moving out on its mission when it was attacked by an estimated 2-company force. During the initial engagement, 1st Lt. Howard was wounded and his weapon destroyed by a grenade explosion. 1st Lt. Howard saw his platoon leader had been wounded seriously and was exposed to fire. Although unable to walk, and weaponless, 1st Lt. Howard unhesitatingly crawled through a hail of fire to retrieve his wounded leader. As 1st Lt. Howard was administering first aid and removing the officer's equipment, an enemy bullet struck 1 of the ammunition pouches on the lieutenant's belt, detonating several magazines of ammunition. 1st Lt. Howard momentarily sought cover and then realizing that he must rejoin the platoon, which had been disorganized by the enemy attack, he again began dragging the seriously wounded officer toward the platoon area.

Through his outstanding example of indomitable courage and bravery, 1st Lt. Howard was able to rally the platoon into an organized defense force. With complete disregard for his safety, 1st Lt. Howard crawled from position to position, administering first aid to the wounded, giving encouragement to the defenders and directing their fire on the encircling enemy. For 3 1/2 hours 1st Lt. Howard's small force and supporting aircraft successfully repulsed enemy attacks and finally were in sufficient control to permit the landing of rescue helicopters. 1st Lt. Howard personally supervised the loading of his men and did not leave the bullet-swept landing zone until all were aboard safely.

1st Lt. Howard's gallantry in action, his complete devotion to the welfare of his men at the risk of his life were in keeping with the highest traditions of the military service and reflect great credit on himself, his unit, and the U.S. Army.

CAPT Thomas J. Hudner, Jr.
U.S. Navy (Ret.) • Korea

"Loyalty: the most important quality a leader must possess. It is true, willing, and unfailing devotion to his cause, his mission, his organization, and his people.

"A leader must be loyal to his juniors (his subordinates), as well as his seniors (his superiors): 'Loyalty down begets loyalty up.' Provided the basic capabilities are there, such an attitude in any organization, military or otherwise, is a guarantor of mission accomplishment.

"And it is loyalty among comrades in the field that succeeds in battle and wins the war."

Rank and organization
Lieutenant (J.G.) U.S. Navy, pilot in Fighter
Squadron 32, attached to U.S.S. Leyte.
Place and date
Chosin Reservoir area of Korea, 4 December 1950.

CITATION

For conspicuous gallantry and intrepidity at the risk of his life above and beyond the call of duty as a pilot in Fighter Squadron 32, while attempting to rescue a squadron mate whose plane, struck by antiaircraft fire and trailing smoke, was forced down behind enemy lines.

Quickly maneuvering to circle the downed pilot and protect him from enemy troops infesting the area, Lt. (J.G.) Hudner risked his life to save the injured flier who was trapped alive in the burning wreckage. Fully aware of the extreme danger in landing on the rough mountainous terrain and the scant hope of escape or survival in subzero temperature, he put his plane down skillfully in a deliberate wheels-up landing in the presence of enemy troops. With his bare hands, he packed the fuselage with snow to keep the flames away from the pilot and struggled to pull him free. Unsuccessful in this, he returned to his crashed aircraft and radioed other airborne planes, requesting that a helicopter be dispatched with an ax and fire extinguisher. He then remained on the spot despite the continuing danger from enemy action and, with the assistance of the rescue pilot, renewed a desperate but unavailing battle against time, cold, and flames.

Lt. (J.G.) Hudner's exceptionally valiant action and selfless devotion to a shipmate sustain and enhance the highest traditions of the U.S. Naval Service.

Einar H. Ingman
U.S. Army • Korea

"In 1953, after the Korean War, I returned home to my wife and little girl. I had been in an Army hospital for two years. I was depressed and thought, 'What am I going to do at twenty-two years old and in my condition?'

"My wife (now of 50 years) said, 'I think you forgot that it isn't what you have lost that counts, it's what you have left.' If you were a blind man, your one eye would be a gift from God. If you were a deaf person, one ear would still allow you to hear your little daughter, the bird's beautiful song, and all the other wonderful sounds. A limp when you walk is better than spending the rest of your life in a wheelchair. As far as the disfigurement of your face, re-member it's what is in your heart that really counts. You should be grateful.'

"I applied for a job the next day, worked for the next thirty-two years, and raised seven children. I have never been depressed again."

Rank and organization
Sergeant (then Cpl.), U.S. Army, Company E,
17th Infantry Regiment, 7th Infantry Division.
Place and date
Near Maltari, Korea, 26 February 1951.

CITATION

Sgt. Ingman, a member of Company E, distinguished himself by conspicuous gallantry and intrepidity above and beyond the call of duty in action against the enemy. The 2 leading squads of the assault platoon of his company, while attacking a strongly fortified ridge held by the enemy, were pinned down by withering fire and both squad leaders and several men were wounded. Cpl. Ingman assumed command, reorganized and combined the 2 squads, then moved from 1 position to another, designating fields of fire and giving advice and encouragement to the men.

Locating an enemy machine gun position that was raking his men with devastating fire, he charged it alone, threw a grenade into the position, and killed the remaining crew with rifle fire. Another enemy machine gun opened fire approximately 15 yards away and inflicted additional casualties to the group and stopped the attack. When Cpl. Ingman charged the second position he was hit by grenade fragments and a hail of fire which seriously wounded him about the face and neck and knocked him to the ground. With incredible courage and stamina, he arose instantly and, using only his rifle, killed the entire guncrew before falling unconscious from his wounds. As a result of the singular action by Cpl. Ingman, the defense of the enemy was broken, his squad secured its objective, and more than 100 hostile troops abandoned their weapons and fled in disorganized retreat.

Cpl. Ingman's indomitable courage, extraordinary heroism, and superb leadership reflect the highest credit on himself and are in keeping with the esteemed traditions of the infantry and the U.S. Army.

Robert R. Ingram
U.S. Navy • Vietnam

"As the years roll by, I find the term 'success' has changed greatly. I find that I have less material needs and a greater need for time to enjoy my family, friends, church, and prayer.

"I find faith to be both the most difficult to obtain and the most rewarding attribute of life. Like courage, you cannot buy it and you are not born with it; it is by the grace of God. You are able to exercise it and build upon it. You are also able to lose it, but God does not forget you. I feel that man needs to be honest, energetic and hard-working, open-minded, empathetic, and humble. If he has these, he will have God in his life, and he will love his fellow man."

CITATION

For conspicuous gallantry and intrepidity at the risk of his life above and beyond the call of duty while serving as Corpsman with Company C, First Battalion, Seventh Marines against elements of a North Vietnam Aggressor (NVA) battalion in Quang Ngai Province Republic of Vietnam on 28 March 1966.

Petty Officer Ingram accompanied the point platoon as it aggressively dispatched an outpost of an NVA battalion. The momentum of the attack rolled off a ridge line down a tree covered slope to a small paddy and a village beyond. Suddenly, the village tree line exploded with an intense hail of automatic rifle fire from approximately 100 North Vietnamese regulars. In mere moments, the platoon ranks were decimated. Oblivious to the danger, Petty Officer Ingram crawled across the bullet spattered terrain to reach a downed Marine. As he administered aid, a bullet went through the palm of his hand.

Calls for "CORPSMAN" echoed across the ridge. Bleeding, he edged across the fire swept landscape, collecting ammunition from the dead and administering aid to the wounded. Receiving two more wounds before realizing the third wound was life-threatening, he looked for a way off the face of the ridge, but again he heard the call for corpsman and again, he resolutely answered. Though severely wounded three times, he rendered aid to those incapable until he finally reached the right flank of the platoon. While dressing the head wound of another corpsman, he sustained his fourth bullet wound. From sixteen hundred hours until just prior to sunset, Petty Officer Ingram pushed, pulled, cajoled, and doctored his Marines. Enduring the pain from his many wounds and disregarding the probability of his demise, Petty Officer Ingram's intrepid actions saved many lives that day.

By his indomitable fighting spirit, daring initiative, and unfaltering dedications to duty, Petty Officer Ingram reflected great credit upon himself and upheld the highest traditions of the United States Naval Service.

Senator Daniel K. Inouye
U.S. Army • WWII

"Soon after my eighteenth birthday, I volunteered to serve in the United States Army. On my day of departure, my father escorted me to my army destination. During that long trip, he said but three sentences. 'This country has been good to us. Whatever you do, do not dishonor this country. Do not dishonor your family.' I have done my best to live up to the words of my father."

CITATION

Second Lieutenant Daniel K. Inouye distinguished himself by extraordinary heroism in action on 21 April 1945, in the vicinity of San Terenzo, Italy. While attacking a defended ridge guarding an important road junction, Second Lieutenant Inouye skillfully directed his platoon through a hail of automatic weapon and small arms fire, in a swift enveloping movement that resulted in the capture of an artillery and mortar post and brought his men to within 40 yards of the hostile force. Emplaced in bunkers and rock formations, the enemy halted the advance with crossfire from three machine guns.

With complete disregard for his personal safety, Second Lieutenant Inouye crawled up the treacherous slope to within five yards of the nearest machine gun and hurled two grenades, destroying the emplacement. Before the enemy could retaliate, he stood up and neutralized a second machine gun nest. Although wounded by a sniper's bullet, he continued to engage other hostile positions at close range until an exploding grenade shattered his right arm. Despite the intense pain, he refused evacuation and continued to direct his platoon until enemy resistance was broken and his men were again deployed in defensive positions.

In the attack, 25 enemy soldiers were killed and eight others captured. By his gallant, aggressive tactics and by his indomitable leadership, Second Lieutenant Inouye enabled his platoon to advance through formidable resistance, and was instrumental in the capture of the ridge.

Second Lieutenant Inouye's extraordinary heroism and devotion to duty are in keeping with the highest traditions of military service and reflect great credit on him, his unit, and the United States Army.

Colonel Joe M. Jackson
U.S. Air Force (Ret.) • Vietnam

"When I was a young boy, I became a Christian. One of the things my mother and my minister taught me was to always do the right thing. I've tried to live up to this requirement, not always being successful—but I've always tried. Major decisions become a lot easier when 'the right thing' is used as a benchmark. How do you know what it is? Of all the options available it is, almost always, the most difficult one to select or to do.

"In addition to always doing the right thing, there are many other attributes that I consider essential. Of those I will address only three. One is integrity. You must be completely honest in everything you do. Your word must be your bond so that you can always be trusted. Another is courage. You must have courage to put all the other required attributes into practice. Courage in everyday life is no different than courage in combat. You must have it to make things happen. And faith is essential if one is to survive those moments when it seems that there is nothing but despair. It is your faith in God that gives you the strength to survive when there is no tangible evidence that you can do so."

Rank and organization
Lieutenant Colonel, U.S. Air Force, 311th Air
Commando Squadron, Da Nang, Republic of Vietnam.
Place and date
Kham Duc, Republic of Vietnam, 12 May 1968.

CITATION

For conspicuous gallantry and intrepidity in action at the risk of his life above and beyond the call of duty. Lt. Col. Jackson distinguished himself as pilot of a C-123 aircraft.

Lt. Col. Jackson volunteered to attempt the rescue of a 3-man USAF Combat Control Team from the special forces camp at Kham Duc. Hostile forces had overrun the forward outpost and established gun positions on the airstrip. They were raking the camp with small arms, mortars, light and heavy automatic weapons, and recoilless rifle fire. The camp was engulfed in flames and ammunition dumps were continuously exploding and littering the runway with debris. In addition, 8 aircraft had been destroyed by the intense enemy fire and 1 aircraft remained on the runway, reducing its usable length to only 2,200 feet. To further complicate the landing, the weather was deteriorating rapidly, thereby permitting only 1 air strike prior to his landing.

Although fully aware of the extreme danger and likely failure of such an attempt, Lt. Col. Jackson elected to land his aircraft and attempt to rescue. Displaying superb airmanship and extraordinary heroism, he landed his aircraft near the point where the combat control team was reported to be hiding. While on the ground, his aircraft was the target of intense hostile fire. A rocket landed in front of the nose of the aircraft but failed to explode. Once the combat control team was aboard, Lt. Col. Jackson succeeded in getting airborne despite the hostile fire directed across the runway in front of his aircraft.

Lt. Col. Jackson's profound concern for his fellowmen, at the risk of his life above and beyond the call of duty, are in keeping with the highest traditions of the U.S. Air Force and reflect great credit upon himself and the Armed Forces of his country.

Colonel Jack H. Jacobs
U.S. Army (Ret.) • Vietnam

"I once had a brigade commander who had a great deal of success in the Army. He was selected to create new units, take command of troubled organizations, and do similar challenging tasks. I never got along with him personally; he was something of an anti-intellectual, had little patience, was narrow-minded and, frankly, a bit bull-headed.

"But he told me something which has stuck with me for decades: 'If you don't know where you're going, any road will take you there.' Never mind that this observation is a quote from Lewis Carroll, the English author; he passed this wisdom to everyone as his own. It is as clear and as useful as advice can be, and while its message is patently obvious to the casual observer, it is astounding how easy it is to overlook. Without an understanding of an objective, without a sense of purpose, efforts are likely to be haphazard, inefficient and, all too often, in vain."

Rank and organization
Captain, U.S. Army, U.S. Army Element,
U.S. Military Assistance Command, Republic of Vietnam.
Place and date
Kien Phong Province, Republic of Vietnam, 9 March 1968.

CITATION

For conspicuous gallantry and intrepidity in action at the risk of his life above and beyond the call of duty. Capt. Jacobs (then 1st Lt.), Infantry, distinguished himself while serving as assistant battalion advisor, 2d Battalion, 16th Infantry, 9th Infantry Division, Army of the Republic of Vietnam.

The 2d Battalion was advancing to contact when it came under intense heavy machine gun and mortar fire from a Viet Cong battalion positioned in well fortified bunkers. As the 2d Battalion deployed into attack formation its advance was halted by devastating fire. Capt. Jacobs, with the command element of the lead company, called for and directed air strikes on the enemy positions to facilitate a renewed attack. Due to the intensity of the enemy fire and heavy casualties to the command group, including the company commander, the attack stopped and the friendly troops became disorganized.

Although wounded by mortar fragments, Capt. Jacobs assumed command of the allied company, ordered a withdrawal from the exposed position and established a defensive perimeter. Despite profuse bleeding from head wounds which impaired his vision, Capt. Jacobs, with complete disregard for his safety, returned under intense fire to evacuate a seriously wounded advisor to the safety of a wooded area where he administered lifesaving first aid. He then returned through heavy automatic weapons fire to evacuate the wounded company commander.

Capt. Jacobs made repeated trips across the fire-swept open rice paddies evacuating wounded and their weapons. On 3 separate occasions, Capt. Jacobs contacted and drove off Viet Cong squads who were searching for allied wounded and weapons, single-handedly killing 3 and wounding several others. His gallant actions and extra-ordinary heroism saved the lives of 1 U.S. advisor and 13 allied soldiers. Through his effort, the allied company was restored to an effective fighting unit and prevented defeat of the friendly forces by a strong and determined enemy.

Capt. Jacobs, by his gallantry and bravery in action in the highest traditions of the military service, has reflected great credit upon himself, his unit, and the U.S. Army.

Psalm 91—The Soldiers' Psalm

He that dwelleth in the secret place of the most High shall abide under the shadow of the Almighty.

I will say of the LORD, He is my refuge and my fortress: my God; in him will I trust.

Surely he shall deliver thee from the snare of the fowler, and from the noisome pestilence.

He shall cover thee with his feathers, and under his wings shalt thou trust: his truth shall be thy shield and buckler.

Thou shalt not be afraid for the terror by night; nor for the arrow that flieth by day;

Nor for the pestilence that walketh in darkness; nor for the destruction that wasteth at noonday.

A thousand shall fall at thy side, and ten thousand at thy right hand; but it shall not come nigh thee.

Only with thine eyes shalt thou behold and see the reward of the wicked.

Because thou hast made the LORD, which is my refuge, even the most High, thy habitation;

There shall no evil befall thee, neither shall any plague come nigh thy dwelling.

For he shall give his angels charge over thee, to keep thee in all thy ways.

They shall bear thee up in their hands, lest thou dash thy foot against a stone.

Thou shalt tread upon the lion and adder: the young lion and the dragon shalt thou trample under feet.

Because he hath set his love upon me, therefore will I deliver him: I will set him on high, because he hath known my name.

He shall call upon me, and I will answer him: I will be with him in trouble; I will deliver him, and honour him.

With long life will I satisfy him, and shew him my salvation.

Major Douglas T. Jacobson
U.S. Marine Corps (Ret.) • WWII

"The game of life is like the game of golf. Keep your eye on the objective. Keep out of the hazards. Stay in the fairway and always remember: Quitters never win, and winners never quit."

Rank and organization
Private First Class, U.S. Marine Corps Reserve,
3d Battalion, 23d Marines, 4th Marine Division.
Place and date
Iwo Jima, Volcano Islands, 26 February 1945.

CITATION

For conspicuous gallantry and intrepidity at the risk of his life above and beyond the call of duty while serving with the 3d Battalion, 23d Marines, 4th Marine Division, in combat against enemy Japanese forces during the seizure of Iwo Jima in the Volcano Island, 26 February 1945.

Promptly destroying a stubborn 20mm. antiaircraft gun and its crew after assuming the duties of a bazooka man who had been killed, Pfc. Jacobson waged a relentless battle as his unit fought desperately toward the summit of Hill 382 in an effort to penetrate the heart of Japanese cross-island defense. Employing his weapon with ready accuracy when his platoon was halted by overwhelming enemy fire on 26 February, he first destroyed 2 hostile machinegun positions, then attacked a large blockhouse, completely neutralizing the fortification before dispatching the 5-man crew of a second pillbox and exploding the installation with a terrific demolitions blast. Moving steadily forward, he wiped out an earth-covered rifle emplacement and, confronted by a cluster of similar emplacements which constituted the perimeter of enemy defenses in his assigned sector, fearlessly advanced, quickly reduced all 6 positions to a shambles, killed 10 of the enemy, and enabled our forces to occupy the strong point.

Determined to widen the breach thus forced, he volunteered his services to an adjacent assault company, neutralized a pillbox holding up its advance, opened fire on a Japanese tank pouring a steady stream of bullets on 1 of our supporting tanks, and smashed the enemy tank's gun turret in a brief but furious action culminating in a single-handed assault against still another blockhouse and the subsequent neutralization of its firepower. By his dauntless skill and valor, Pfc. Jacobson destroyed a total of 16 enemy positions and annihilated approximately 75 Japanese, thereby contributing essentially to the success of his division's operations against this fanatically defended outpost of the Japanese Empire.

His gallant conduct in the face of tremendous odds enhanced and sustained the highest traditions of the U.S. Naval Service.

Captain Thomas G. Kelley
U.S. Navy (Ret.) • Vietnam

"Anything's possible as long as no one cares who gets the credit.

"Knowing the right thing to do is usually easy. Doing the right thing is often very tough.

"Leading soldiers, sailors, airmen, and marines is the toughest, yet noblest job that we can do. Their well-being is in our hands and if we don't take that responsibility, then we don't belong in the position."

Rank and organization

Lieutenant Commander, U.S. Navy, River Assault Division 152.

Place and date

Ong Muong Canal, Kien Hoa province, Republic of Vietnam, 15 June 1969.

CITATION

For conspicuous gallantry and intrepidity at the risk of his life above and beyond the call of duty in the afternoon while serving as commander of River Assault Division 152 during combat operations against enemy aggressor forces.

Lt. Comdr. (then Lt.) Kelley was in charge of a column of 8 river assault craft, which were extracting 1 company of U.S. Army infantry troops on the east bank of the Ong Muong Canal in Kien Hoa province, when 1 of the armored troop carriers reported a mechanical failure of a loading ramp. At approximately the same time, Viet Cong forces opened fire from the opposite bank of the canal. After issuing orders for the crippled troop carrier to raise its ramp manually and for the remaining boats to form a protective cordon around the disabled craft, Lt. Comdr. Kelley realizing the extreme danger to his column and its inability to clear the ambush site until the crippled unit was repaired, boldly maneuvered the monitor in which he was embarked to the exposed side of the protective cordon in direct line with the enemy's fire, and ordered the monitor to commence firing. Suddenly, an enemy rocket scored a direct hit on the coxswain's flat, the shell penetrating the thick armor plate, and the explosion spraying shrapnel in all directions.

Sustaining serious head wounds from the blast, which hurled him to the deck of the monitor, Lt. Cmdr. Kelley disregarded his severe injuries and attempted to continue directing the other boats. Although unable to move from the deck or to speak clearly into the radio, he succeeded in relaying his commands through 1 of his men until the enemy attack was silenced and the boats were able to move to an area of safety. Lt. Comdr. Kelley's brilliant leadership, bold initiative, and resolute determination served to inspire his men and provide the impetus needed to carry out the mission after he was medically evacuated by helicopter.

His extraordinary courage under fire, and his selfless devotion to duty sustain and enhance the finest traditions of the U.S. Naval Service.

Thomas J. Kinsman
U.S. Army • Vietnam

"I try to treat people as I would like them to treat me. I try to pull my own weight in our society. Finally, I try to raise my children to believe in God and treat others with respect. If I can do these things, I will have accomplished what God put me here to do."

Rank and organization
Specialist Fourth Class, U.S. Army, Company B,
3d Battalion, 60th Infantry, 9th Infantry Division.
Place and date
Near Vinh Long, Republic of Vietnam, 6 February 1968.

CITATION

For conspicuous gallantry and intrepidity in action at the risk of his life above and beyond the call of duty, Sp4c. Kinsman (then Pfc.) distinguished himself in action in the afternoon while serving as a rifleman with Company B on a reconnaissance-in-force mission. As his company was proceeding up a narrow canal in armored troops carriers, it came under sudden and intense rocket, automatic weapons, and small-arms fire from a well-entrenched Viet Cong force. The company immediately beached and began assaulting the enemy bunker complex.

Hampered by exceedingly dense undergrowth which limited visibility to 10 meters, a group of 8 men became cut off from the main body of the company. As they were moving through heavy enemy fire to effect a link-up, an enemy soldier in a concealed position hurled a grenade into their midst. Sp4c. Kinsman immediately alerted his comrades of the danger, then unhesitatingly threw himself on the grenade and blocked the explosion with his body. As a result of his courageous action, he received severe head and chest wounds. Through his indomitable courage, complete disregard for his personal safety and profound concern for his fellow soldiers, Sp4c. Kinsman averted loss of life and injury to the other 7 men of his element.

Sp4c. Kinsman's extraordinary heroism at the risk of his life, above and beyond the call of duty, are in keeping with the highest traditions of the military service and reflect great credit upon himself, his unit, and the U.S. Army.

George C. Lang
U.S. Army • Vietnam

"As a young boy my parents always encouraged me to do what was right. In life, most of us are taught what's right and what's wrong. My advice would be the same: Do what you know is right. Knowing what's right and doing what's right can be difficult, but you must be true to yourself. I would also stress the importance of faith in God. With faith, you will find the strength to fulfill God's plan for your life."

Rank and organization
Specialist Fourth Class, U.S. Army, Company A,
4th Battalion, 47th Infantry, 9th Infantry Division.
Place and date
Kien Hoa province, Republic of Vietnam, 22 February 1969.

CITATION

For conspicuous gallantry and intrepidity in action at the risk of his life above and beyond the call of duty. Sp4c. Lang, Company A, was serving as a squad leader when his unit, on a reconnaissance-in-force mission, encountered intense fire from a well-fortified enemy bunker complex.

Sp4c. Lang observed an emplacement from which heavy fire was coming. Unhesitatingly, he assaulted the position and destroyed it with hand grenades and rifle fire. Observing another emplacement approximately 15 meters to his front, Sp4c. Lang jumped across a canal, moved through heavy enemy fire to within a few feet of the position, and eliminated it, again using hand grenades and rifle fire. Nearby, he discovered a large cache of enemy ammunition. As he maneuvered his squad forward to secure the cache, they came under fire from yet a third bunker. Sp4c. Lang immediately reacted, assaulted his position, and destroyed it with the remainder of his grenades.

After returning to the area of the arms cache, his squad again came under heavy enemy rocket and automatic weapons fire from 3 sides and suffered 6 casualties. Sp4c. Lang was 1 of those seriously wounded. Although immobilized and in great pain, he continued to direct his men until his evacuation was ordered over his protests.

The sustained extraordinary courage and selflessness exhibited by this soldier over an extended period of time were an inspiration to his comrades and are in keeping with the highest traditions of the U.S. Army.

Colonel William Lawley
U.S. Air Force (Ret.) • WWII

"I was blessed and am honored to have served my country for more than thirty years as an officer in the United States Air Force. I want to stress that I am not a Medal of Honor *winner*—no one seeks to become a *winner*. I am a *recipient* of the Medal of Honor, who served with the 364th Bombardment Squadron during World War II as an Army Air Corps pilot flying B-17 aircraft.

"I will be the first to say, there are many brave men and women who deserve to be recognized as heroes. We were all doing a job that we had to do. If Harry Mason, my bombardier, and the other members of my crew had not helped me on that fateful mission, we would have all been killed. We all had to work together and with the help of God, we made it back.

"In life we are not promised that things will be easy or that we will not experience difficulties and challenges. In fact, there are times in life when the situations and circumstances you are involved in may be extremely difficult. During difficult times, your character will be tested. Your response to these difficulties will determine your character.

"Every American must remember the sacrifices made by those who died to protect our freedom! Those individuals who paid the supreme sacrifice were willing to give up their tomorrows so we could have our todays.

"I would urge every young American to trust in God and have faith in Him. Live a life committed to God, country, and family. Always do what you know is right. Be honest, because integrity and character are profoundly important."

Rank and organization
First Lieutenant, U.S. Army Air Corps,
364th Bomber Squadron, 305th Bomber Group.
Place and date
Over Europe, 20 February 1944.

CITATION

For conspicuous gallantry and intrepidity in action above and beyond the call of duty, 20 February 1944, while serving as pilot of a B-17 aircraft on a heavy bombardment mission over enemy-occupied continental Europe.

Coming off the target, he was attacked by approximately 20 enemy fighters, shot out of formation, and his plane severely crippled. Eight crewmembers were wounded, the copilot was killed by a 20-mm. shell. One engine was on fire, the controls shot away, and 1st Lt. Lawley seriously and painfully wounded about the face. Forcing the copilot's body off the controls, he brought the plane out of a steep dive, flying with his left hand only. Blood covered the instruments and windshield, and visibility was impossible. With a full bomb load the plane was difficult to maneuver, and bombs could not be released because the racks were frozen.

After the order to bail out had been given, 1 of the waist gunners informed the pilot that 2 crewmembers were so severely wounded that it would be impossible for them to bail out. With the fire in the engine spreading, the danger of an explosion was imminent. Because of the helpless condition of his wounded crewmembers, 1st Lt. Lawley elected to remain with the ship and bring them to safety if it was humanly possible, giving the other crewmembers the option of bailing out. Enemy fighters again attacked, but by using masterful evasive action, he managed to lose them. One engine again caught on fire and was extinguished by skillful flying. 1st Lt. Lawley remained at his post, refusing first aid until he collapsed from sheer exhaustion caused by loss of blood, shock, and the energy he had expended in keeping control of his plane. He was revived by the bombardier and again took over the controls. Coming over the English coast, 1 engine ran out of gasoline and had to be feathered. Another engine started to burn and continued to do so until a successful crash landing was made on a small fighter base.

Through his heroism and exceptional flying skill, 1st Lt. Lawley rendered outstanding distinguished and valorous service to our nation.

First Awards in Nation

The first formal system for rewarding acts of individual gallantry by the nation's fighting men was established by General George Washington on August 7, 1782. Designed to recognize "any singularly meritorious action," the award consisted of a purple cloth heart. Records show that only three persons received the award: Sergeant Elijah Churchill, Sergeant William Brown, and Sergeant Daniel Bissel Jr.

The Badge of Military Merit, as it was called, fell into oblivion until 1932, when General Douglas MacArthur, then Army Chief of Staff, pressed for its revival. Officially reinstituted on February 22, 1932, the now familiar Purple Heart was at first an Army award, given to those who had been wounded in World War I or who possessed a Meritorious Service Citation Certificate. In 1943, the order was amended to include personnel of the Navy, Marine Corps, and Coast Guard. Coverage was eventually extended to include all services and "any civilian national" wounded while serving with the Armed Forces.

Peter C. Lemon
U.S. Army • Vietnam

"Each night, when I tuck my children into bed, we read, discuss their day, and then I leave them with this last message: 'Have sweet dreams tonight, dream about everything you love in life, never forget how special you are and how special those people around you are, never forget how much you are loved by me and by God. I believe in you, care for you immensely, and trust you. Always remember TRC. And what does that mean?' They respond, 'Make the Right Choice.' Then they give me an example.

"You see, in life, there are only three choices: the wrong, the best, and the right choice. But only one choice is appropriate or correct, and that is TRC.

"Decision making is similar to any other training. The more you train and train correctly, the more proficient you become. If you start in life, or even end up in life (because it's never too late), training to make the right choices, then when an important major decision comes your way, you are prepared to make the right choice without hesitation."

Rank and organization
Sergeant, U.S. Army, Company E,
2d Battalion, 8th Cavalry, 1st Cavalry Division.
Place and date
Tay Ninh province, Republic of Vietnam, 1 April 1970.

CITATION

For conspicuous gallantry and intrepidity in action at the risk of his life above and beyond the call of duty. Sgt. Lemon (then Sp4c.), Company E, distinguished himself while serving as an assistant machine gunner during the defense of Fire Support Base Illingworth.

When the base came under heavy enemy attack, Sgt. Lemon engaged a numerically superior enemy with machine gun and rifle fire from his defensive position until both weapons malfunctioned. He then used hand grenades to fend off the intensified enemy attack launched in his direction. After eliminating all but 1 of the enemy soldiers in the immediate vicinity, he pursued and disposed of the remaining soldier in hand-to-hand combat. Despite fragment wounds from an exploding grenade, Sgt. Lemon regained his position, carried a more seriously wounded comrade to an aid station, and, as he returned, was wounded a second time by enemy fire. Disregarding his personal injuries, he moved to his position through a hail of small arms and grenade fire.

Sgt. Lemon immediately realized that the defensive sector was in danger of being overrun by the enemy and unhesitatingly assaulted the enemy soldiers by throwing hand grenades and engaging in hand-to-hand combat. He was wounded yet a third time, but his determined efforts successfully drove the enemy from the position. Securing an operable machine gun, Sgt. Lemon stood atop an embankment fully exposed to enemy fire and placed effective fire upon the enemy until he collapsed from his multiple wounds and exhaustion. After regaining consciousness at the aid station, he refused medical evacuation until his more seriously wounded comrades had been evacuated. Sgt. Lemon's gallantry and extraordinary heroism, are in keeping with the highest traditions of the military service and reflect great credit on him, his unit, and the U.S. Army.

Command Sergeant Major
Gary L. Littrell
U.S. Army (Ret.) • Vietnam

"By virtue of a general order, the Department of Defense has declared me a hero. Every young man and woman of the United States can be my hero. To be my hero, do what's right. You know right from wrong. You know it is wrong to use drugs and you know it is wrong to bring unwanted children into this world. Never succumb to peer pressure. If it is right, do it and you will be my hero.

"My advice for life is: Always do what is right. You should strive to be totally honest. Your word is your bond. Stand up for what you believe in even if it is difficult, and never ask someone to do something you are not willing to do."

Rank and organization
Sergeant First Class, U.S. Army, Advisory Team 21,
11 Corps Advisory Group.
Place and date
Kontum province, Republic of Vietnam, 4-8 April 1970.

CITATION
For conspicuous gallantry and intrepidity in action at the risk of

his life above and beyond the call of duty. Sfc. Littrell, U.S. Military Assistance Command, Vietnam, Advisory Team 21, distinguished himself while serving as a Light Weapons Infantry Advisor with the 23d Battalion, 2d Ranger Group, Republic of Vietnam Army, near Dak Seang.

After establishing a defensive perimeter on a hill on April 4, the battalion was subjected to an intense enemy mortar attack which killed the Vietnamese commander, 1 advisor, and seriously wounded all the advisors except Sfc. Littrell. During the ensuing 4 days, Sfc Littrell exhibited near superhuman endurance as he single-handedly bolstered the besieged battalion. Repeatedly abandoning positions of relative safety, he directed artillery and air support by day and marked the unit's location by night, despite the heavy, concentrated enemy fire.

His dauntless will instilled in the men of the 23d Battalion a deep desire to resist. Assault after assault was repulsed as the battalion responded to the extraordinary leadership and personal example exhibited by Sfc. Littrell as he continuously moved to those points most seriously threatened by the enemy, redistributed ammunition, strengthened faltering defenses, cared for the wounded, and shouted encouragement to the Vietnamese in their own language.

When the beleaguered battalion was finally ordered to withdraw, numerous ambushes were encountered. Sfc. Littrell repeatedly prevented widespread disorder by directing air strikes to within 50 meters of their position. Through his indomitable courage and complete disregard for his safety, he averted excessive loss of life and injury to the members of the battalion.

The sustained extraordinary courage and selflessness displayed by Sfc. Littrell over an extended period of time were in keeping with the highest traditions of the military service and reflect great credit on him and the U.S. Army.

Major General James E. Livingston
U.S. Marine Corps (Ret.) • Vietnam

"Significance comes with caring—caring about the people who you are involved with on a daily basis. Through caring, you become significant. Significance comes from achievements—not achievements in the sense of monetary awards but how your actions affect the achievements of others. If those around you, as a result of your personal understanding and efforts, become better persons and contribute beyond their expectations, you have been significant.

"Significance is your personal legacy. What beyond worldly goals will be your lasting legacy? It can be as simple as reminding a child of his/her responsibility or making a personal commitment to changing the total course of society or history. Significance is by deeds and acts, and less of words."

Rank and organization
Captain, U.S. Marine Corps, Company E,
2d Battalion, 4th Marines, 9th Marine Amphibious Brigade.
Place and date
Dai Do, Republic of Vietnam, 2 May 1968.

CITATION

For conspicuous gallantry and intrepidity at the risk of his life above and beyond the call of duty while serving as Commanding Officer, Company E, in action against enemy forces. Company E launched a determined assault on the heavily fortified village of Dai Do, which had been seized by the enemy on the preceding evening isolating a marine company from the remainder of the battalion. Skillfully employing screening agents, Capt. Livingston maneuvered his men to assault positions across 500 meters of dangerous open rice paddy while under intense enemy fire. Ignoring hostile rounds impacting near him, he fearlessly led his men in a savage assault against enemy emplacements within the village. While adjusting supporting arms fire, Capt. Livingston moved to the points of heaviest resistance, shouting words of encouragement to his marines, directing their fire, and spurring the dwindling momentum of the attack on repeated occasions. Although twice painfully wounded by grenade fragments, he refused medical treatment and courageously led his men in the destruction of over 100 mutually supporting bunkers, driving the remaining enemy from their positions, and relieving the pressure on the stranded marine company.

As the 2 companies consolidated positions and evacuated casualties, a third company passed through the friendly lines launching an assault on the adjacent village of Dinh To, only to be halted by a furious counterattack of an enemy battalion. Swiftly assessing the situation and disregarding the heavy volume of enemy fire, Capt. Livingston boldly maneuvered the remaining effective men of his company forward, joined forces with the heavily engaged marines, and halted the enemy's counterattack. Wounded a third time and unable to walk, he steadfastly remained in the dangerously exposed area, deploying his men to more tenable positions and supervising the evacuation of casualties. Only when assured of the safety of his men, did he allow himself to be evacuated.

Capt. Livingston's gallant actions uphold the highest traditions of the Marine Corps and the U.S. Naval Service.

Sergeant First Class Jose M. Lopez
U.S. Army (Ret.) • WWII

"I believe the only way to survive in life is with family and faith. In war—during the rough times or easier times—I have always relied on my faith, and it was my faith that pulled me through.

"Time with my family is precious. In addition to spending time with my family, I also pray, attend church, and do everything possible to keep my faith alive.

"Without faith, without family—where would we be?"

Rank and organization
Sergeant, U.S. Army, 23d Infantry, 2d Infantry Division.
Place and date
Near Krinkelt, Belgium, 17 December 1944.

CITATION

On his own initiative, he carried his heavy machinegun from Company K's right flank to its left, in order to protect that flank which was in danger of being overrun by advancing enemy infantry supported by tanks. Occupying a shallow hole offering no protection above his waist, he cut down a group of 10 Germans. Ignoring enemy fire from an advancing tank, he held his position and cut down 25 more enemy infantry attempting to turn his flank. Glancing to his right, he saw a large number of infantry swarming in from the front.

Although dazed and shaken from enemy artillery fire which had crashed into the ground only a few yards away, he realized that his position soon would be outflanked. Again, alone, he carried his machinegun to a position to the right rear of the sector; enemy tanks and infantry were forcing a withdrawal. Blown over backward by the concussion of enemy fire, he immediately reset his gun and continued his fire. Single-handed he held off the German horde until he was satisfied his company had effected its retirement. Again he loaded his gun on his back and in a hail of small arms fire, he ran to a point where a few of his comrades were attempting to set up another defense against the onrushing enemy. He fired from this position until his ammunition was exhausted. Still carrying his gun, he fell back with his small group to Krinkelt.

Sgt. Lopez's gallantry and intrepidity, on seemingly suicidal missions in which he killed at least 100 of the enemy, were almost solely responsible for allowing Company K to avoid being enveloped, to withdraw successfully, and to give other forces coming up in support time to build a line which repelled the enemy drive.

Jack H. Lucas
U.S. Marine Corps • WWII

"Regardless of race, economic standing, or what part of the country you are from, men should stand tall, without reservation or preservation of life to fulfill the mission to protect this beautiful country of ours. We Marines look out for one another. We stand together for the Corps and country.

"Give of yourself completely and believe in God. Jesus Christ said in chapter 15 and verse 13 of the gospel of John: 'No greater love hath any man that he give his life for his friends.' Without hesitation, that's what this seventeen-year-old Marine did and was willing to do on Iwo Jima for my fellow Marines. But for and by the grace of God, I survived."

Rank and organization
Private First Class, U.S. Marine Corps Reserve,
1st Battalion, 26th Marines, 5th Marine Division.
Place and date
Iwo Jima, Volcano Islands, 20 February 1945.

CITATION

For conspicuous gallantry and intrepidity at the risk of his life above and beyond the call of duty while serving with the 1st Battalion, 26th Marines, 5th Marine Division, during action against enemy Japanese forces on Iwo Jima, Volcano Islands, 20 February 1945.

While creeping through a treacherous, twisting ravine which ran in close proximity to a fluid and uncertain frontline on D-plus-1 day, Pfc. Lucas and 3 other men were suddenly ambushed by a hostile patrol which savagely attacked with rifle fire and grenades. Quick to act when the lives of the small group were endangered by 2 grenades which landed directly in front of them, Pfc. Lucas unhesitatingly hurled himself over his comrades upon 1 grenade and pulled the other under him, absorbing the whole blasting forces of the explosions in his own body in order to shield his companions from the concussion and murderous flying fragments.

By his inspiring action and valiant spirit of self-sacrifice, he not only protected his comrades from certain injury or possible death but also enabled them to rout the Japanese patrol and continue the advance.

His exceptionally courageous initiative and loyalty reflect the highest credit upon Pfc. Lucas and the U.S. Naval Service.

Allen J. Lynch
U.S. Army • Vietnam

"Both my mother and father were Christians who loved the Lord Jesus. Both gave me a deep religious faith. Even when I'm away from God, I know that my sins are forgiven. This knowledge has given me faith in myself. If God can forgive me and has faith in me, then so do I. This faith has sustained me through many times of doubt.

"This quote from Teddy Roosevelt is my creed. 'It is not the critic who counts, not the man who points out how the strong man stumbled, or when the doer of deeds could have done better. The credit belongs to the man who is actually in the arena; whose face is marred by dirt and sweat and blood; who strives valiantly, who errs and comes short again and again; who knows the great enthusiasms, and spends himself in a worthy cause; who, at the best, knows in the end the triumph of his achievements, and who, at the worst, if he fails, at least fails while daring greatly, so that his place shall never be with those cold and timid souls who know neither victory nor defeat.'"

Rank and organization
Sergeant, U.S. Army, Company D, 1st Battalion (Airmobile),
12th Cavalry, 1st Cavalry Division (Airmobile).

Place and date
Near My An (2), Binh Dinh province,
Republic of Vietnam, 15 December 1967.

CITATION

For conspicuous gallantry and intrepidity in action at the risk of his life above and beyond the call of duty. Sgt. Lynch (then Sp4c.) distinguished himself while serving as a radio telephone operator with Company D.

While serving in the forward element on an operation near the village of My An, his unit became heavily engaged with a numerically superior enemy force. Quickly and accurately assessing the situation, Sgt. Lynch provided his commander with information which subsequently proved essential to the unit's successful actions. Observing 3 wounded comrades Lying exposed to enemy fire, Sgt. Lynch dashed across 50 meters of open ground through a withering hail of enemy fire to administer aid. Reconnoitering a nearby trench for a covered position to protect the wounded from intense hostile fire, he killed 2 enemy soldiers at point blank range. With the trench cleared, he unhesitatingly returned to the fire-swept area 3 times to carry the wounded men to safety.

When his company was forced to withdraw by the superior firepower of the enemy, Sgt. Lynch remained to aid his comrades at the risk of his life rather than abandon them. Alone, he defended his isolated position for 2 hours against the advancing enemy. Using only his rifle and a grenade, he stopped them just short of his trench, killing 5. Again, disregarding his safety in the face of withering hostile fire, he crossed 70 meters of exposed terrain 5 times to carry his wounded comrades to a more secure area. Once he had assured their comfort and safety, Sgt. Lynch located the counterattacking friendly company to assist in directing the attack and evacuating the 3 casualties.

His gallantry at the risk of his life is in the highest traditions of the military service, Sgt. Lynch has reflected great credit on himself, the 12th Cavalry, and the U.S. Army.

Colonel Walter J. Marm
U.S. Army (Ret.) • Vietnam

"God is love. My parents were excellent role models for my three sisters and me. They believed the family that prays together stays together. Prayer, faith, and church were an integral part of our upbringing. My strong religious faith has helped me every day of my life. I firmly believe that God does not put more in your rucksack than you can carry; although, sometimes you think He does. God has a plan for each of us and we are important to Him...born in His image and likeness. Life is precious and we must live each day as if it could be our last. Stay close to Him...always.

"There is no greater love than to lay down your life for a friend. In combat, we were prepared to die for our buddies, our unit, and our country. General Patton once said, 'The more you sweat in training, the less you bleed in war.' Continue to train at every opportunity, even in combat. A well-trained unit is cohesive and is ready to 'take on the world.'"

Rank and organization
First Lieutenant (then 2d Lt.), U.S. Army, Company A,
1st Battalion, 7th Cavalry, 1st Cavalry Division (Airmobile).
Place and date
Vicinity of la Drang Valley, Republic of Vietnam,
14 November 1965.

CITATION

For conspicuous gallantry and intrepidity at the risk of life above and beyond the call of duty. As a platoon leader in the 1st Cavalry Division (Airmobile), 1st Lt. Marm demonstrated indomitable courage during a combat operation.

His company was moving through the valley to relieve a friendly unit surrounded by an enemy force of estimated regimental size. 1st Lt. Marm led his platoon through withering fire until they were finally forced to take cover. Realizing that his platoon could not hold very long, and seeing four enemy soldiers moving into his position, he moved quickly under heavy fire and annihilated all 4. Then, seeing that his platoon was receiving intense fire from a concealed machine gun, he deliberately exposed himself to draw its fire. Thus locating its position, he attempted to destroy it with an antitank weapon. Although he inflicted casualties, the weapon did not silence the enemy fire. Quickly, disregarding the intense fire directed on him and his platoon, he charged 30 meters across open ground, and hurled grenades into the enemy position, killing some of the 8 insurgents manning it.

Although severely wounded, when his grenades were expended, armed with only a rifle, he continued the momentum of his assault on the position and killed the remainder of the enemy. 1st Lt. Marm's selfless actions reduced the fire on his platoon, broke the enemy assault, and rallied his unit to continue toward the accomplishment of this mission.

1st Lt. Marm's gallantry on the battlefield and his extraordinary intrepidity at the risk of his life are in the highest traditions of the U.S. Army and reflect great credit upon himself and the Armed Forces of his country.

Robert D. Maxwell
U.S. Army • WWII

"Much of our success in life is determined by how we handle our anxieties and fears of the unknown future. Because of fear, we may be hesitant to step out into avenues of opportunity. Our anxieties may cause us to miss much of life's good things.

"We can draw consolation from two teachings of Jesus: 1) Let Him handle anxieties (Matt. 6:25-34); and 2) Fear can be displaced by love (1 John 4:17-18). When we have the love that comes from God, we can overcome the anxieties that accompany very frightening situations. Our own concern for self-preservation, though very important to us, is less than our concern for others we love. This is why people often risk their life to save others (John 15:13)."

Technician Fifth Grade, U.S. Army,
7th Infantry, 3d Infantry Division.
Place and date
Near Besancon, France, 7 September 1944.

CITATION

For conspicuous gallantry and intrepidity at risk of life above and beyond the call of duty on 7 September 1944, near Besancon, France.

Technician 5th Grade Maxwell and 3 other soldiers, armed only with .45 caliber automatic pistols, defended the battalion observation post against an overwhelming onslaught by enemy infantrymen in approximately platoon strength, supported by 20mm. flak and machinegun fire, who had infiltrated through the battalion's forward companies and were attacking the observation post with machinegun, machine pistol, and grenade fire at ranges as close as 10 yards. Despite a hail of fire from automatic weapons and grenade launchers, Technician 5th Grade Maxwell aggressively fought off advancing enemy elements and, by his calmness, tenacity, and fortitude, inspired his fellows to continue the unequal struggle. When an enemy hand grenade was thrown in the midst of his squad, Technician 5th Grade Maxwell unhesitatingly hurled himself squarely upon it, using his blanket and his unprotected body to absorb the full force of the explosion.

This act of instantaneous heroism permanently maimed Technician 5th Grade Maxwell, but saved the lives of his comrades in arms and facilitated maintenance of vital military communications during the temporary withdrawal of the battalion's forward headquarters.

THE SHIELD OF FAITH

I believe that faith is the most important aspect of humanity. "Faith is being sure of what we hope for and certain of what we do not see" (Hebrews 11:1 NIV). It takes faith in a higher authority than ourselves for progress to take place in our lives. Many, if not most, of America's great leaders expressed a trust in God as an influence on their success. Those gallant men who officiated at the birth of our nation trusted and had a faith in God as the Higher Power to watch over the struggling colonies. We see the results of their faith and works and those of many great leaders throughout the centuries, which culminated in the development of this great nation that has always offered liberty to the world's oppressed. Since our beginning, we have fought wars endeavoring to maintain that liberty throughout the free world.

Without faith the fighting forces of our nation cannot perform their duty. They must trust in the authority above them, from the commander-in-chief down to their squad leader. For example, when danger threatens the very existence of the combat soldier, he must rely on his training, experience, fellow soldiers, and that Higher Power—God—to survive. Every combat veteran can say, "I know, I've been there."

Faith, even if just newly found, has the ability to change lives. I met a retired veteran a few years ago who told me his story. His military career included a life of alcohol abuse. Over time he became an alcoholic, a disease that is permanent and unrelenting. On December 7, 1976, he "kicked the habit" and joined with others who had a similar problem and started in the Alcoholic's Anonymous program. It's hard for anyone with a "macho" image, who is self-sufficient and also a determined person, to believe in any force greater than himself. The man and his wife were invited to attend church. While visiting with a few of the men from the congregation, he met three veterans in the parking lot.

One of these veterans served as a Marine Raider in World War II and also survived the desperate fighting and winter at the Chosin

Reservoir in Korea. The former Marine was the father of the pastor of the church. Another of the veterans was a former Army Air Corps B-17 radio operator and upper turret gunner. This veteran's plane was shot down over Germany. He was seriously injured when he made a parachute landing on the concrete road of a small German town. He spent the remainder of the war as a POW in Stalag 17. The other veteran had received the Medal of Honor. His infantry career ended with the blast from a German grenade in France.

After meeting and visiting these veterans, he realized that these men were for real. As a result, he and his wife were immersed in Christian love. Our friendship continued over the years. Our "alcoholic" friend had finally found something in which to believe. He found the power that would help him overcome and control the craving monster that had dominated his life. He no longer had to face his problem alone.

He now had the assurance that this new life included faith in a Mediator who would intercede with God about his requests and needs. Fortunately this experience, this faith is available to all of us.

—*Robert Maxwell*

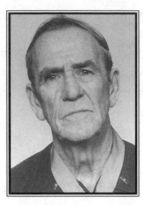

First Sergeant David H. McNerney
U.S. Army (Ret.) • Vietnam

"I would offer this advice to young men and women who will be our future leaders. Every person should have some tangible goal that guides or influences him or her with utter disregard for the intangibles.

"God, ideals, beliefs, and a sense of belonging to something good and great, can be an everlasting motivation that enables a person to produce, to the maximum of their capabilities, a pride in themselves and their fellow citizens.

"For the young people of America, I would also offer this thought: I have read that ultimately the only thing that each of us has in this world is his or her name. What else identifies us? Our name should be one of our most cherished possessions. We are the sole master of that name. What we do or fail to do with that name is our responsibility.

"Finally, I believe that knowledge is extremely important, especially historical knowledge. From this, we know where we were and where we are going. A knowledge of the United States helps us form our opinions of who we are, what has been accomplished, and what we can be."

Rank and organization
First Sergeant, U.S. Army, Company A,
1st Battalion, 8th Infantry, 4th Infantry Division.
Place and date
polei Doc, Republic of Vietnam, 22 March 1967.

CITATION

1st Sgt. McNerney distinguished himself when his unit was attacked by a North Vietnamese battalion near polei Doc.

Running through the hail of enemy fire to the area of heaviest contact, he was assisting in the development of a defensive perimeter when he encountered several enemy at close range. He killed the enemy but was painfully injured when blown from his feet by a grenade. In spite of this injury, he assaulted and destroyed an enemy machinegun position that had pinned down 5 of his comrades beyond the defensive line.

Upon learning his commander and artillery forward observer had been killed, he assumed command of the company. He adjusted artillery fire to within 20 meters of the position in a daring measure to repulse enemy assaults. When the smoke grenades used to mark the position were gone, he moved into a nearby clearing to designate the location to friendly aircraft. In spite of enemy fire, he remained exposed until he was certain the position was spotted and then climbed into a tree and tied the identification panel to its highest branches. Then he moved among his men readjusting their position, encouraging the defenders, and checking the wounded. As the hostile assaults slackened, he began clearing a helicopter landing site to evacuate the wounded.

When explosives were needed to remove large trees, he crawled outside the relative safety of his perimeter to collect demolition material from abandoned rucksacks. Moving through a fusillade of fire, he returned with the explosives that were vital to the clearing of the landing zone. Disregarding the pain of his injury and refusing medical evacuation, 1st Sgt. McNerney remained with his unit until the next day when the new commander arrived.

First Sgt. McNerney's outstanding heroism and leadership were inspirational to his comrades. His actions were in keeping with the highest traditions of the U.S. Army and reflect great credit upon himself and the Armed Forces of his country.

MOH Awarded to:

87 African-Americans

41 Hispanic-Americans

31 Asian-Americans

22 Native-Americans

The first African-American recipient was William Carney. He was awarded the Medal of Honor for his actions on July 18, 1863 at Fort Wagner, SC. Seven African Americans along with 22 Asian-Americans received the Medal of Honor for their service during WWII. Their citations prove that these men courageously joined the ranks of those who distinguished themselves with extraordinary valor, above and beyond the call of duty. Many of the Japanese Americans volunteered from internment camps, where their families had been relocated at the outbreak of war.

In the 20th century, five American Indians have been among those soldiers to be distinguished by receiving the Medal of Honor. These warriors exhibited extraordinary bravery in the face of the enemy and, in two cases, made the ultimate sacrifice for their country.

Representing their tribes were First Lieutenant Jack C. Montgomery—a Cherokee from Oklahoma; First Lieutenant Ernest Childers—a Creek from Oklahoma; Second Lieutenant Van Barfoot—a Choctaw from Mississippi; Corporal Mitchell Red Cloud Jr.—a Winnebago from Wisconsin; and Private First Class Charles George—a Cherokee from North Carolina.

Gino J. Merli
U.S. Army • WWII

"I left high school early, without graduating, to serve my nation in WWII. My family was a patriotic family; my three brothers and only sister all served in the military.

"I survived the landing on Omaha Beach, fought through Normandy, and the Huerigen Forest, and I was seriously wounded during the Battle of the Bulge. After I returned home, I went back to school to get my high school diploma.

"If you were to ask my wife, she would describe me as a peaceful, dedicated family man. I guess that's true, but I also know, even if you love peace, you still have to be willing to fight for what you believe in. I believe freedom is worth fighting and dying for.

"I have a great respect for the veteran. The veteran paid a great price for freedom. President Calvin Coolidge once said. 'The nation which forgets its defenders will itself be forgotten.'

"My advice for life would include: Continue your education. Give the honor due those who served our nation in uniform. Always be honest and maintain the highest moral integrity. If you always try to serve others, you will have a blessed life. Finally, make a commitment to love God, country, and family."

Private First Class, U.S. Army,
18th Infantry, 1st Infantry Division.
Place and date
Near Sars la Bruyere, Belgium, 45 September 1944.

CITATION

He was serving as a machine gunner in the vicinity of Sars la Bruyere, Belgium, on the night of 45 September 1944, when his company was attacked by a superior German force. Its position was overrun, and he was surrounded when our troops were driven back by overwhelming numbers and firepower. Disregarding the fury of the enemy fire concentrated on him, he maintained his position, covering the withdrawal of our riflemen and breaking the force of the enemy pressure.

His assistant machine gunner was killed and the position captured; the other 8 members of the section were forced to surrender. Pfc. Merli slumped down beside the dead assistant gunner and feigned death. No sooner had the enemy group withdrawn then he was up and firing in all directions. Once more his position was taken, and the captors found 2 apparently lifeless bodies. Throughout the night Pfc. Merli stayed at his weapon. By daybreak the enemy had suffered heavy losses, and as our troops launched an assault, asked for a truce. Our negotiating party, who accepted the German surrender, found Pfc. Merli still at his gun. On the battlefield lay 52 enemy dead, 19 of whom were directly in front of the gun.

Pfc. Merli's gallantry and courage, and the losses and confusion that he caused the enemy, contributed materially to our victory.

Colonel Lewis L. Millett
U.S. Army (Ret.) • Korea

"Every 4th of July our family would meet on the beaches of Maine. As a young boy I loved to listen to the stories about family members who served our nation in uniform. Our family has a proud military tradition. We have served in every one of our nation's major conflicts. My uncle fought and was wounded in World War I. He was my hero.

"I believe everyone in America should be willing to serve and, if necessary, fight for freedom. We must always remember, we must never forget, freedom is not free!

"My advice to our future leaders is: Never give up. Character and integrity are important. Stand up for what you believe in. Finally, the most important rule of leadership is never ask or order someone to do something that you are not willing to do."

Rank and organization
Captain, U.S. Army, Company E, 27th Infantry Regiment.
Place and date
Vicinity of Soam-Ni, Korea, 7 February 1951.

CITATION

Capt. Millett, Company E, distinguished himself by conspicuous gallantry and intrepidity above and beyond the call of duty in action.

While personally leading his company in an attack against a strongly held position, he noted that the 1st Platoon was pinned down by small-arms, automatic, and antitank fire. Capt. Millett ordered the 3d Platoon forward, placed himself at the head of the 2 platoons, and, with fixed bayonet, led the assault up the fire-swept hill. In the fierce charge, Capt. Millett bayoneted 2 enemy soldiers and boldly continued on, throwing grenades, clubbing and bayoneting the enemy, while urging his men forward by shouting encouragement. Despite vicious opposing fire, the whirlwind hand-to-hand assault carried to the crest of the hill.

His dauntless leadership and personal courage so inspired his men that they stormed into the hostile position and used their bayonets with such lethal effect that the enemy fled in wild disorder. During this fierce onslaught, Capt. Millett was wounded by grenade fragments but refused evacuation until the objective was taken and firmly secured.

The superb leadership, conspicuous courage, and consummate devotion to duty demonstrated by Capt. Millett were directly responsible for the successful accomplishment of a hazardous mission and reflect the highest credit on himself and the heroic traditions of the military service.

Hiroshi H. Miyamura
U.S. Army • Korea

"As you and I know, our country has become great and has flourished because we are and have been a God-fearing country. I wish that our youth today and the future generations to come will continue to believe in God and try to live with their fellow man. I truly believe that if the youth of today and future generations would learn to judge a person by his or her actions and personality as an individual, then we will be a much happier nation.

"I believe that my learning of the Lord as a child helped me throughout my life, most especially in the military while in Korea. For only God helped me through that night of April 24, 1951. I could not have made it without His guidance."

Rank and organization
Corporal, U.S. Army, Company H,
7th Infantry Regiment, 3rd Infantry Division.
Place and date
Near Taejon-ni, Korea, 24 and 25 April 1951.

CITATION

Cpl. Miyamura, a member of Company H, distinguished himself by conspicuous gallantry and intrepidity above and beyond the call of duty in action against the enemy. On the night of 24 April, Company H was occupying a defensive position when the enemy fanatically attacked threatening to overrun the position. Cpl. Miyamura, a machine gun squad leader, aware of the imminent danger to his men, unhesitatingly jumped from his shelter wielding his bayonet in close hand-to-hand combat killing approximately 10 of the enemy. Returning to his position, he administered first aid to the wounded and directed their evacuation. As another savage assault hit the line, he manned his machine gun and delivered withering fire until his ammunition was expended. He ordered the squad to withdraw while he stayed behind to render the gun inoperative. He then bayoneted his way through infiltrated enemy soldiers to a second gun emplacement and assisted in its operation.

When the intensity of the attack necessitated the withdrawal of the company, Cpl. Miyamura ordered his men to fall back while he remained to cover their movement. He killed more than 50 of the enemy before his ammunition was depleted and he was severely wounded. He maintained his magnificent stand despite his painful wounds, continuing to repel the attack until his position was overrun. When last seen, he was fighting ferociously against an overwhelming number of enemy soldiers.

Cpl. Miyamura's indomitable heroism and consummate devotion to duty reflect the utmost glory on himself and uphold the illustrious traditions on the military service.

Colonel Robert J. Modrzejewski
U.S. Marine Corps (Ret.) • Vietnam

"I used to tell my young Marine recruits when I was a Battalion Commander that every day will be a test; and every time you fail to do what you know is right, it weakens your character and creates distrust among those who rely on you to hold up your end of the effort. In combat, the battlefield is no place for you to be learning your job.

"For many years, my religious beliefs were somewhat superficial. I became used to thinking about everything except God. Following a serious medical operation, my relationship with God changed completely. Since that time, I have tried to give something back to my church and community. My life now is God, family, and country. It took a crisis for me to get my priorities in order, but with God, all things are possible."

Rank and organization
Major (then Capt.), U.S. Marine Corps, Company K, 3d Battalion, 4th Marines, 3d Marine Division, FMF.
Place and date
Republic of Vietnam, 15 to 18 July 1966.

CITATION

For conspicuous gallantry and intrepidity at the risk of his life above and beyond the call of duty.

On 15 July, during Operation HASTINGS, Company K was landed in an enemy-infested jungle area to establish a blocking position at a major enemy trail network. Shortly after landing, the company encountered a reinforced enemy platoon in a well-organized, defensive position. Maj. Modrzejewski led his men in the successful seizure of the enemy redoubt, which contained large quantities of ammunition and supplies. That evening, a numerically superior enemy force counterattacked in an effort to retake the vital supply area, thus setting the pattern of activity for the next 2 1/2 days.

In the first series of attacks, the enemy assaulted repeatedly in overwhelming numbers, but each time was repulsed by the gallant marines. The second night, the enemy struck in battalion strength, and Maj. Modrzejewski was wounded in this intensive action which was fought at close quarters. Although exposed to enemy fire, and despite his painful wounds, he crawled 200 meters to provide critically needed ammunition to an exposed element of his command and was constantly present wherever the fighting was heaviest, despite numerous casualties, a dwindling supply of ammunition, and the knowledge that they were surrounded, he skillfully directed artillery fire to within a few meters of his position and courageously inspired the efforts of his company in repelling the aggressive enemy attack.

On 18 July, Company K was attacked by a regimental-size enemy force. Although his unit was vastly outnumbered and weakened by the previous fighting, Maj. Modrzejewski reorganized his men and calmly moved among them to encourage and direct their efforts to heroic limits as they fought to overcome the vicious enemy onslaught. Again he called in air and artillery strikes at close range with devastating effect on the enemy, which together with the bold and determined fighting of the men of Company K, repulsed the fanatical attack of the larger North Vietnamese force. His unparalleled personal heroism and indomitable leadership inspired his men to a significant victory over the enemy force and reflected great credit upon himself, the Marine Corps, and the U.S. Naval Service.

Jack C. Montgomery
U.S. Army • WWII

"Some things I've learned—after 80 years: Live one day at a time. Always do your best. Go the extra mile. Learn from mistakes. Don't let failure discourage you. Be forgiving, both of yourself and of others. Always respect authority. Be honest—sincere and well-balanced. Above all else, make it a habit to praise the Lord!"

———

Rank and organization
First Lieutenant, U.S. Army, 45th Infantry Division.
Place and date
Near Padiglione, Italy, 22 February 1944.

CITATION
For conspicuous gallantry and intrepidity at risk of life above and beyond the call of duty on 22 February 1944, near Padiglione, Italy.

Two hours before daybreak a strong force of enemy infantry established themselves in 3 echelons at 50 yards, 100 yards, and 300 yards, respectively, in front of the rifle platoons commanded by 1st

Lt. Montgomery. The closest position, consisting of 4 machineguns and 1 mortar, threatened the immediate security of the platoon position. Seizing an Ml rifle and several hand grenades, 1st Lt. Montgomery crawled up a ditch to within hand grenade range of the enemy. Then climbing boldly onto a little mound, he fired his rifle and threw his grenades so accurately that he killed 8 of the enemy and captured the remaining 4.

Returning to his platoon, he called for artillery fire on a house, in and around which he suspected that the majority of the enemy had entrenched themselves. Arming himself with a carbine, he proceeded along the shallow ditch, as withering fire from the riflemen and machinegunners in the second position was concentrated on him. He attacked this position with such fury that 7 of the enemy surrendered to him, and both machineguns were silenced. Three German dead were found in the vicinity later that morning.

1st Lt. Montgomery continued boldly toward the house, 300 yards from his platoon position. It was now daylight, and the enemy observation was excellent across the flat open terrain which led to 1st Lt. Montgomery's objective. When the artillery barrage had lifted, 1st Lt. Montgomery ran fearlessly toward the strongly defended position. As the enemy started streaming out of the house, 1st Lt. Montgomery, unafraid of treacherous snipers, exposed himself daringly to assemble the surrendering enemy and send them to the rear. His fearless, aggressive, and intrepid actions that morning, accounted for a total of 11 enemy dead, 32 prisoners, and an unknown number of wounded. That night, while aiding an adjacent unit to repulse a counterattack, he was struck by mortar fragments and seriously wounded.

The selflessness and courage exhibited by 1st Lt. Montgomery in alone attacking 3 strong enemy positions inspired his men to a degree beyond estimation.

Captain Raymond G. Murphy
U.S. Marine Corps (Ret.) • Korea

"My creed or code of conduct for life is that I always respect others and try to be honest and positive with them. The spiritual advice that I would give is this: I pray to God every day and I try to make Him the foundation of my life."

Rank and organization
Second Lieutenant, U.S. Marine Corps Reserve, Company A, 1st Battalion, 5th Marines, 1st Marine Division (Rein.).
Place and date
Korea, 3 February 1953.

CITATION
For conspicuous gallantry and intrepidity at the risk of his life above and beyond the call of duty as a platoon commander of Company A, in action against enemy aggressor forces.

Although painfully wounded by fragments from an enemy mortar shell while leading his evacuation platoon in support of assault units attacking a cleverly concealed and well-entrenched hostile force occupying commanding ground, 2d Lt. Murphy steadfastly refused medical aid and continued to lead his men up a hill through a withering barrage of hostile mortar and small-arms fire, skillfully maneuvering his force from one position to the next and shouting words of encouragement. Undeterred by the increasing intense enemy fire, he immediately located casualties as they fell and made several trips up and down the fire-swept hill to direct evacuation teams to the wounded, personally carrying many of the stricken marines to safety.

When reinforcements were needed by the assaulting elements, 2d Lt. Murphy employed part of his unit as support and, during the ensuing battle, personally killed 2 of the enemy with his pistol. With all the wounded evacuated and the assaulting units beginning to disengage, he remained behind with a carbine to cover the movement of friendly forces off the hill and, though suffering intense pain from his previous wounds, seized an automatic rifle to provide more firepower when the enemy reappeared in the trenches.

After reaching the base of the hill, he organized a search party and again ascended the slope for a final check on missing marines, locating and carrying the bodies of a machine gun crew back down the hill. Wounded a second time while conducting the entire force to the line of departure through a continuing barrage of enemy small-arms, artillery, and mortar fire, he again refused medical assistance until assured that every one of his men, including all casualties, had preceded him to the main lines.

His resolute and inspiring leadership, exceptional fortitude, and great personal valor reflect the highest credit upon 2d Lt. Murphy and enhance the finest traditions of the U.S. Naval Service.

Colonel Charles P. Murray, Jr.
U.S. Army (Ret.) • WWII

"During my years in the military service and on my travels since then, I have visited in a number of countries around the world. I have enjoyed seeing their historic places, their great cathedrals, their palaces, their museums, their cities, and their countryside. But I am always glad to be home again because there is nowhere on this earth like America.

"We may not be perfect. However, we must agree that, as Americans, we have been richly blessed. There is no country on earth that is better than ours. There is no country on earth that offers the advantages and opportunities we enjoy.

"It is urgent that the young people of this nation learn to appreciate the freedoms which they enjoy, the freedoms which have been provided to them by others. They should show their love for America, show respect for their flag and other people, and do what they can to correct failures of character and other weaknesses which permeate our society.

"My advice to the youth of America, in preparing to take on the burden of leadership positions in this great nation, is to take maximum advantage of every opportunity that comes your way through education and training to advance yourself. Moreover, you should search for ways to do this, not just wait for an opportunity to come knocking. And in all things, always do your best. Beyond this, work hard to stretch your limits. The nation is waiting for you to take charge."

———————

Rank and organization
First Lieutenant, U.S. Army, Company C,
30th Infantry, 3d Infantry Division.
Place and date
Near Kaysersberg, France, 16 December 1944.

CITATION
For commanding Company C, 30th Infantry, displaying supreme courage and heroic initiative near Kaysersberg, France, on 16 December 1944, while leading a reinforced platoon into enemy territory.

Descending into a valley beneath hilltop positions held by our troops, he observed a force of 200 Germans pouring deadly mortar, bazooka, machinegun, and small arms fire into an American battalion occupying the crest of the ridge. The enemy's position in a sunken road, though hidden from the ridge, was open to a flank attack by 1st Lt. Murray's patrol, but he hesitated to commit so small a force to battle with the superior and strongly disposed enemy. Crawling out ahead of his troops to a vantage point, he called by radio for artillery fire. His shells bracketed the German force, but when he was about to correct the range his radio went dead. He returned to his patrol, secured grenades and a rifle to launch them, and went back to his self-appointed outpost. His first shots disclosed his position; the enemy directed heavy fire against him as he methodically fired his missiles into the narrow defile.

Again he returned to his patrol. With an automatic rifle and ammunition, he once more moved to his exposed position. Burst after burst he fired into the enemy, killing 20, wounding many others, and completely disorganizing its ranks, which began to withdraw. He prevented the removal of 3 German mortars by knocking out a truck. By that time a mortar had been brought to his support. 1st Lt. Murray directed fire of this weapon, causing further casualties and confusion in the German ranks.

Calling on his patrol to follow, he then moved out toward his original objective, possession of a bridge and construction of a road-block. He captured 10 Germans in foxholes. An eleventh, while pretending to surrender, threw a grenade which knocked him to the ground, inflicting 8 wounds. Though suffering and bleeding profusely, he refused to return to the rear until he had chosen the spot for the block and had seen his men correctly deployed.

By his single-handed attack on an overwhelming force and by his intrepid and heroic fighting, 1st Lt. Murray stopped a counterattack, established an advance position against formidable odds, and provided an inspiring example for the men of his command.

One Woman Awarded the MOH

When the Civil War started, the Union Army wouldn't hire women doctors, so Walker volunteered as a nurse in Washington's Patent Office Hospital and treated wounded soldiers at the Battle of Bull Run in Virginia. In 1862, she received an Army contract appointing her as an assistant surgeon with the 52nd Ohio Infantry.

The first woman doctor to serve with the Army Medical Corps, Mary Walker cared for sick and wounded troops in Tennessee at Chickamauga and in Georgia during the Battle of Atlanta.

Confederate troops captured her on April 10, 1864, and held her until the sides exchanged prisoners of war on Aug. 12, 1864. The Army nominated Walker for the Medal of Honor for her wartime service, and President Andrew Johnson signed the citation on Nov. 11, 1865, and she received the award on Jan. 24, 1866. Her citation cites her wartime service, but not specifically valor in combat.

Her citation cites her wartime service. Her citation reads in part that she "devoted herself with much patriotic zeal to the sick and wounded soldiers, both in the field and hospitals, to the detriment of her own health. She has also endured hardships as a prisoner of war for four months in a Southern prison while acting as contract surgeon."

The U.S. Postal Service honored Civil War Dr. Mary E. Walker, the only woman awarded the Medal of Honor, with a 20-cent first-class postage stamp in 1982.

Colonel Reginald Myers
U.S. Marine Corps (Ret.) • Korea

"It seems to me that all too frequently today you find that our youth have no direction for their life's beliefs. I'm not sure if this is the fault of the youth or of their parents who fail in their leadership role and example for our youth. Due to our desire for a 'good life,' we all too frequently ignore our responsibilities of bringing up our children, and therefore, let them 'wander' on their own or let their philosophy be developed by others.

"Our youth must be brought up to believe in themselves. They must be taught to dedicate their effort to do right. They must always be faithful to the right philosophy of life. They should not be left to wander by themselves."

Rank and organization
Major, U.S. Marine Corps, 3d Battalion,
1st Marines, 1st Marine Division, (Rein.).
Place and date
Near Hagaru-ri, Korea, 29 November 1950.

CITATION

For conspicuous gallantry and intrepidity at the risk of his life above and beyond the call of duty as executive officer of the 3d Battalion, in action against enemy aggressor forces. Assuming command of a composite unit of Army and Marine service and headquarters elements totaling approximately 250 men, during a critical stage in the vital defense of the strategically important military base at Hagaru-ri, Maj. Myers immediately initiated a determined and aggressive counterattack against a well-entrenched and cleverly concealed enemy force numbering an estimated 4,000. Severely handicapped by a lack of trained personnel and experienced leaders in his valiant efforts to regain maximum ground prior to daylight, he persisted in constantly exposing himself to intense, accurate, and sustained hostile fire in order to direct and supervise the employment of his men and to encourage and spur them on in pressing the attack.

Inexorably moving forward up the steep, snow-covered slope with his depleted group in the face of apparently insurmountable odds, he concurrently directed artillery and mortar fire with superb skill and although losing 170 of his men during 14 hours of raging combat in subzero temperatures, continued to reorganize his unit and spearhead the attack which resulted in 600 enemy killed and 500 wounded.

By his exceptional and valorous leadership throughout, Maj. Myers contributed directly to the success of his unit in restoring the perimeter. His resolute spirit of self-sacrifice and unfaltering devotion to duty enhance and sustain the highest traditions of the U.S. Naval Service.

Colonel Robert B. Nett
U.S. Army (Ret.) • WWII

"I like to refer to the quotes from the great General George S. Patton, 'Sweat saves blood' and 'Wars may be fought with weapons, but they are won by men. It is the spirit of the man who follows and of the man who leads that gains victory.'

"I feel we must use some guidelines from the successful leaders of our past. I want students to know that education is an essential element in becoming good citizens. Abraham Lincoln said, 'A country with no regard for its past will do little worth remembering in the future.' In addition to education, they must also learn to appreciate others and the views of others. The youth of today are the strength of tomorrow."

Rank and organization
Captain (then Lieutenant), U.S. Army,
Company E, 305th Infantry, 77th Infantry Division.
Place and date
Near Cognon, Leyte, Philippine Islands, 14 December 1944.

CITATION

He commanded Company E in an attack against a reinforced enemy battalion which had held up the American advance for 2 days from its entrenched positions around a 3-story concrete building. With another infantry company and armored vehicles, Company E advanced against heavy machinegun and other automatic weapons fire with Lt. Nett spearheading the assault against the strongpoint.

During the fierce hand-to-hand encounter which ensued, he killed 7 deeply entrenched Japanese with his rifle and bayonet and, although seriously wounded, gallantly continued to lead his men forward, refusing to relinquish his command. Again he was severely wounded, but, still unwilling to retire, pressed ahead with his troops to assure the capture of the objective. Wounded once more in the final assault, he calmly made all arrangements for the resumption of the advance, turned over his command to another officer, and then walked unaided to the rear for medical treatment.

By his remarkable courage in continuing forward through sheer determination despite successive wounds, Lt. Nett provided an inspiring example for his men and was instrumental in the capture of a vital strongpoint.

Captain Beryl Newman
U.S. Army (Ret.) • WWII

"Would I do it all over again? Yes, I would defend my country because I love it so much. I did not face the enemy alone for the glory of doing so but to save my men that I loved and were under my command. It was my place to protect them.

"Yes, I would do the same things all over again. I fought for my country so that people would have a free place to live. We can do all things through the strength that God gives us. Jesus was the ultimate possibility thinker. He taught us to see what needs to be done and to do what is right. If everybody lived by the Ten Commandments, there would be no more wars."

Rank and organization
First Lieutenant, U.S. Army, 133d Infantry, 34th Infantry Division.
Place and date
Near Cisterna, Italy, 26 May 1944.

CITATION
For conspicuous gallantry and intrepidity above and beyond the call of duty on 26 May 1944.

Attacking the strongly held German Anzio-Nettuno defense line near Cisterna, Italy, 1st Lt. Newman, in the lead of his platoon, was suddenly fired upon by 2 enemy machineguns located on the crest of a hill about 100 yards to his front. The 4 scouts with him immediately hit the ground, but 1st Lt. Newman remained standing in order to see the enemy positions and his platoon then about 100 yards behind. Locating the enemy nests, 1st Lt. Newman called back to his platoon and ordered 1 squad to advance to him and the other to flank the enemy to the right. Then, still standing upright in the face of the enemy machinegun fire, 1st Lt. Newman opened up with his tommygun on the enemy nests. From this range, his fire was not effective in covering the advance of his squads, and 1 squad was pinned down by the enemy fire.

Seeing that his squad was unable to advance, 1st Lt. Newman, in full view of the enemy gunners and in the face of their continuous fire, advanced alone on the enemy nests. He returned their fire with his tommygun and succeeded in wounding a German in each of the nests. The remaining 2 Germans fled from the position into a nearby house. Three more enemy soldiers then came out of the house and ran toward a third machinegun. 1st Lt. Newman, still relentlessly advancing toward them, killed 1 before he reached the gun, the second before he could fire it. The third fled for his life back into the house. Covering his assault by firing into the doors and windows of the house, 1st Lt. Newman, boldly attacking by himself, called for the occupants to surrender to him. Gaining the house, he kicked in the door and went inside. Although armed with rifles and machine pistols, the 11 Germans there, apparently intimidated, surrendered to the lieutenant without further resistance, 1st Lt. Newman, single-handed, had silenced 3 enemy machineguns, wounded 2 Germans, killed 2 more, and took 11 prisoners.

This demonstration of sheer courage, bravery, and willingness to close with the enemy even in the face of such heavy odds, instilled into these green troops the confidence of veterans and reflects the highest traditions of the U.S. Armed Forces.

Chief Warrant Officer 4
Michael J. Novosel
U.S. Army (Ret.) • Vietnam

"As a warrant officer, I am not often asked for guidance. I am an individual from the trenches. I let others make grand plans and strategies. If the planning and strategic thinking fail to bring success, I and others like me will do our best to salvage the situation while the 'higher ups' take their bows for success.

"I have only one rule to guide me in my endeavors and that is 'BE DEPENDABLE.' In that way, I can be a blessing to my commander—he knows any mission he might assign me will be assured of success. He can take that assurance to the bank."

Rank and organization
Chief Warrant Officer, U.S. Army, 82d Medical Detachment, 45th Medical Company, 68th Medical Group.
Place and date
Kien Tuong Province, Republic of Vietnam, 2 October 1969.

CITATION
For conspicuous gallantry and intrepidity in action at the risk of

his life above and beyond the call of duty. CWO Novosel, 82d Medical Detachment, distinguished himself while serving as commander of a medical evacuation helicopter. He unhesitatingly maneuvered his helicopter into a heavily fortified and defended enemy training area where a group of wounded Vietnamese soldiers were pinned down by a large enemy force. Flying without gunship or other cover and exposed to intense machinegun fire, CWO Novosel was able to locate and rescue a wounded soldier. Since all communications with the beleaguered troops had been lost, he repeatedly circled the battle area, flying at low level under continuous heavy fire, to attract the attention of the scattered friendly troops. This display of courage visibly raised their morale, as they recognized this as a signal to assemble for evacuation.

On 6 occasions, he and his crew were forced out of the battle area by the intense enemy fire, only to circle and return from another direction to land and extract additional troops. Near the end of the mission, a wounded soldier was spotted close to an enemy bunker. Fully realizing that he would attract a hail of enemy fire, CWO Novosel nevertheless attempted the extraction by hovering the helicopter backward. As the man was pulled on aboard, enemy automatic weapons opened fire at close range, damaged the aircraft, and wounded CWO Novosel. He momentarily lost control of the aircraft but quickly recovered and departed under the withering enemy fire. In all, 15 extremely hazardous extractions were performed in order to remove wounded personnel. As a direct result of his selfless conduct, the lives of 29 soldiers were saved.

The extraordinary heroism displayed by CWO Novosel was an inspiration to his comrades in arms and reflect great credit on him, his unit, and the U.S. Army.

George H. O'Brien
U.S. Marine Corps • Korea

"I would urge young people today to be straight forward and honest with their fellow man, treating all as equals and to realize that God has a plan for each of our lives. Place your faith and trust in Him, asking His guidance and you will learn that you can do many things you thought impossible."

Rank and organization
Second Lieutenant, U.S. Marine Corps Reserve, Company H, 3d Battalion, 7th Marines, 1st Marine Division (Rein.).
Place and date
Korea, 27 October, 1952.

CITATION

For conspicuous gallantry and intrepidity at the risk of his life above and beyond the call of duty as a rifle platoon commander of Company H, in action against enemy aggressor forces.

With his platoon subjected to an intense mortar and artillery bombardment while preparing to assault a vitally important hill position on the main line of resistance which had been overrun by a numerically superior enemy force on the preceding night, 2d Lt O'Brien leaped from his trench when the attack signal was given and, shouting for his men to follow, raced across an exposed saddle and up the enemy-held hill through a virtual hail of deadly small-arms, artillery, and mortar fire. Although shot through the arm and thrown to the ground by hostile automatic-weapons fire as he neared the well-entrenched enemy position, he bravely regained his feet, waved his men onward, and continued to spearhead the assault, pausing only long enough to go to the aid of a wounded marine. Encountering the enemy at close range, he proceeded to hurl handgrenades into the bunkers and, utilizing his carbine to best advantage in savage hand-to-hand combat, succeeded in killing at least 3 of the enemy.

Struck down by the concussion of grenades on 3 occasions during the subsequent action, he steadfastly refused to be evacuated for medical treatment and continued to lead his platoon in the assault for a period of nearly 4 hours, repeatedly encouraging his men and maintaining superb direction of the unit. With the attack halted, he set up a defense with his remaining forces to prepare for a counterattack, personally checking each position, attending to the wounded, and expediting their evacuation. When a relief of the position was effected by another unit, he remained to cover the withdrawal and to assure that no wounded were left behind.

By his exceptionally daring and forceful leadership in the face of overwhelming odds, 2d Lt. O'Brien served as a constant source of inspiration to all who observed him and was greatly instrumental in the recapture of a strategic position on the main line of resistance. His indomitable determination and valiant fighting spirit reflect the highest credit upon himself and enhance the finest traditions of the U.S. Naval Service.

Robert E. O'Malley
U.S. Marine Corps • Vietnam

"My father's most frequent advice to my brothers, and my sister and me while we were growing up was: 'Always be honest and honorable.' I've tried to do that. They are good words to live by."

Rank and organization
Sergeant (then Cpl.), U .S. Marine Corps, Company 1,
3d Battalion, 3d Marine Regiment, 3d Marine Division (Rein).
Place and date
Near An Cu'ong 2, South Vietnam, 18 August 1965.

CITATION

For conspicuous gallantry and intrepidity in action against the communist (Viet Cong) forces at the risk of his life above and beyond the call of duty.

While leading his squad in the assault against a strongly entrenched enemy force, his unit came under intense small-arms fire. With complete disregard for his personal safety, Sgt. O'Malley raced across an open rice paddy to a trench line where the enemy forces were located. Jumping into the trench, he attacked the Viet Cong with his rifle and grenades, and singly killed 8 of the enemy. He then led his squad to the assistance of an adjacent marine unit which was suffering heavy casualties. Continuing to press forward, he reloaded his weapon and fired with telling effect into the enemy emplacement. He personally assisted in the evacuation of several wounded marines, and again regrouping the remnants of his squad, he returned to the point of the heaviest fighting.

Ordered to an evacuation point by an officer, Sgt. O'Malley gathered his besieged and badly wounded squad and boldly led them under fire to a helicopter for withdrawal. Although 3 times wounded in this encounter and facing imminent death from a fanatic and determined enemy, he steadfastly refused evacuation and continued to cover his squad's boarding of the helicopters while, from an exposed position, he delivered fire against the enemy until his wounded men were evacuated. Only then, with his last mission accomplished, did he permit himself to be removed from the battlefield.

By his valor, leadership, and courageous efforts in behalf of his comrades, he served as an inspiration to all who observed him, and reflected the highest credit upon the Marine Corps and the U.S. Naval Service.

Nicholas Oresko
U.S. Army • WWII

"In life we encounter many obstacles; even when life is good, it can still be tough. You should stay with it; it is amazing how much you are able to do at any given moment.

"Your best laid plans are subject to interruption and adjustment, so be flexible and ready to make changes. Also remember, prayers are answered.

To the young, I say—'Stay in school and fully complete your education,' because without it, life will be a struggle."

Rank and organization
Master Sergeant, U.S. Army, Company C,
302d Infantry, 94th Infantry Division.
Place and date
Near Tettington, Germany, 23 January 1945.

CITATION

M/Sgt. Oresko was a platoon leader with Company C, in an attack against strong enemy positions. Deadly automatic fire from the flanks pinned down his unit. Realizing that a machinegun in a nearby bunker must be eliminated, he swiftly worked ahead alone, braving bullets, which struck about him, until close enough to throw a grenade into the German position. He rushed the bunker and, with pointblank rifle fire, killed all the hostile occupants who survived the grenade blast. Another machinegun opened up on him, knocking him down and seriously wounding him in the hip. Refusing to withdraw from the battle, he placed himself at the head of his platoon to continue the assault.

As withering machinegun and rifle fire swept the area, he struck out alone in advance of his men to a second bunker. With a grenade, he crippled the dug-in machinegun defending this position and then wiped out the troops manning it with his rifle, completing his second self-imposed, 1-man attack. Although weak from loss of blood, he refused to be evacuated until assured the mission was successfully accomplished.

Through quick thinking, indomitable courage, and unswerving devotion to the attack in the face of bitter resistance and while wounded, M /Sgt. Oresko killed 12 Germans, prevented a delay in the assault, and made it possible for Company C to obtain its objective with minimum casualties.

Colonel Mitchell Paige
U.S. Marine Corps (Ret.) WWII

"My parents and teachers instilled in me a devout love of God, family, and country. When I left home after high school to enlist in the Marines, my God-fearing mother admonished me to 'Just trust in God always.' Six years later, right after the fierce battle on Guadalcanal, I emptied the contents of my combat pack, and because of my burned hands, I gingerly picked up my pocket New Testament which included the Psalms and Proverbs. The page providentially opened to Proverbs 3:5-6: 'Trust in the Lord with all your heart, and lean not on your own understanding. In all your ways acknowledge Him and He will direct your paths.'

"My greatest earthly honor was being awarded the Congressional Medal of Honor. My highest honor—bar none—is, as a sinner, to know Jesus Christ as my Lord and Savior and through Him to know the peace of heart that passes all human understanding. I believe any American with firm moral convictions and courage to defend them at any cost is able to defend himself and maintain his integrity. Valor and patriotism, virtues of the highest order, are part of our beliefs which we must never forget. Since its birth in 1776, our great nation has proudly proclaimed the cherished slogan, 'IN GOD WE TRUST.' Someone once said, 'The evidence of God's presence far outweighs the proof of His absence.'"

236

Rank and organization
Platoon Sergeant, U.S. Marine Corps.
Place and date
Solomon Islands, 26 October 1942

CITATION

For extraordinary heroism and conspicuous gallantry in action above and beyond the call of duty while serving with a company of Marines in combat against enemy Japanese forces in the Solomon Islands on 26 October 1942.

When the enemy broke through the line directly in front of his position, P/Sgt. Paige, commanding a machinegun section with fearless determination, continued to direct the fire of his gunners until all his men were either killed or wounded. Alone, against the deadly hail of Japanese shells, he fought with his gun and when it was destroyed, took over another, moving from gun to gun, never ceasing his withering fire against the advancing hordes until reinforcements finally arrived. Then, forming a new line, he dauntlessly and aggressively led a bayonet charge, driving the enemy back and preventing a breakthrough in our lines.

His great personal valor and unyielding devotion to duty were in keeping with the highest traditions of the U.S. Naval Service.

TRUST IN THE LORD

When I left home to enlist in the Marine Corps, my mother told me "All I want you to do is trust in the God, don't try to figure out everything by yourself and God will show you the way." I joined the Marines in 1936 after I finished high school. During the battle of Guadalcanal, I was a platoon Sergeant in H Company, 2nd Battalion, 7th Regiment, 1st Marines. Following the initial landing on Guadalcanal, the Marines captured the Japanese airfield and named it Henderson Field.

On October 26th, 1942, I was involved in the crucial battle that prevented the enemy from over-running and recapturing Henderson Field. My 33-man platoon was positioned on a ridge within clear observation of the Japanese and Japanese artillery fire. Throughout the day of October 25th, we waited with great anticipation for night to fall. We knew the enemy was aware of our position. Marine patrols had reported that a large body of enemy troops was moving toward our position. Two battalions of the Japanese 124th Infantry Regiment and one Battalion of the 4th Infantry—comprised of about 2,500 to 3,000 enemy soldiers—were moving into position to assault the ridge.

Although the platoon was under strength, we knew we had to hold the ridge at all costs. I moved up and down the line to encourage every Marine and to tell them to hold their fire until the enemy could be seen clearly. Very early in the morning on the 26th of October, we began to see movement below us. As the battle erupted, the enemy advanced to the ridge and our position. The battle became a life and death struggle all along the ridge. After the first wave, a second wave came and the enemy was close to controlling the ridge. Every member of my platoon was either killed or wounded. It was a living hell. I continued to fire my machine gun until the barrel began to steam. In front of me, there was a large pile of dead Japanese soldiers. I ran along the ridge from gun to gun trying to keep them firing, but at each emplacement, I found only dead bodies.

Once when I was running between the gun positions, an enemy soldier rushed at me and with a thrust of his bayonet cut the fingers of my hand. I pushed his rifle aside and using my K-Bar knife, I killed the enemy soldier. A few minutes later, I found myself racing an enemy soldier to one of the gun emplacements. I got there first, but I discovered that the weapon was not loaded. As I tried desperately to pull the bolt back on the machine gun, a strange feeling came over me. I was unable to lean forward; it was like my body was in a vise. Even with that, I felt relaxed and had no fear. All of a sudden, I felt a release from the vise-like hold, and I fell forward over the gun. At the exact moment that this was happening, the enemy soldier had fired his full 30-round magazine at me. I felt the heat and the blast of those bullets pass close to my face and chin. Had I been able to lean forward and pull the bolt back on the machine gun, the bullets would have hit me in the head. I realized I had been spared and protected by an invisible shield.

As dawn broke on the 26th of October, the platoon, now only 26 men, rallied to charge and counterattack. As we ran toward the enemy, I was carrying a red-hot machine gun cradled across my bare arms and hands. With the counterattack, the remaining enemy withdrew. Returning to my gun position, I began to empty the contents of my combat pack to find my Bible. Because my hands were burned by the hot metal barrel of the machine gun, I was unable to hold the Bible. It fell to the ground and it opened to the third chapter of Proverbs. It opened to the chapter and verse given as an admonition from my mother when I left home in 1936. "Trust in the Lord with all your heart and lean not to your own understanding. In all your ways acknowledge Him and He will direct your path." Another Marine ran up to me. He told me later that I was standing there talking to myself, saying, "Mom, Mom." I know the greatest earthly honor that can be given to an American fighting man is the Medal of Honor. But my highest honor, bar none, is to know Jesus Christ as my Lord and Savior."

—*Mitchell Paige*

Command Sergeant Major
Robert M. Patterson
U.S. Army (Ret.) • Vietnam

"If I was to offer my advice for life or a code of conduct for life, I would stress the importance of integrity. I believe that integrity is an extremely important character trait. You are not born with integrity; it has to be learned. Once it's lost, it's almost impossible to regain. As long as you have integrity, everyone you deal with will recognize that you have it, and they will respect you and what you stand for. As leaders, we have two sacred trusts: The first sacred trust is freedom; the second sacred trust is our sons and our daughters, our future leaders. We are responsible for teaching our future leaders—our sons and daughters—the importance of integrity, and we must do it by example."

Rank and organization
Sergeant, U.S. Army, Troop B, 2d Squadron, 17th Cavalry.
Place and date
Near La Chu, Republic of Vietnam, 6 May 1968.

CITATION

For conspicuous gallantry and intrepidity in action at the risk of his life above and beyond the call of duty. Sgt. Patterson (then Sp4c.) distinguished himself while serving as a fire team leader of the 3d Platoon, Troop B, during an assault against a North Vietnamese Army battalion which was entrenched in a heavily fortified position.

When the leading squad of the 3d Platoon was pinned down by heavy interlocking automatic weapon and rocket propelled grenade fire from 2 enemy bunkers, Sgt. Patterson and the 2 other members of his assault team moved forward under a hail of enemy fire to destroy the bunkers with grenade and machinegun fire. Observing that his comrades were being fired on from a third enemy bunker covered by enemy gunners in 1-man spider holes, Sgt. Patterson, with complete disregard for his safety and ignoring the warning of his comrades that he was moving into a bunker complex, assaulted and destroyed the position. Although exposed to intensive small arm and grenade fire from the bunkers and their mutually supporting emplacements. Sgt. Patterson continued his assault upon the bunkers which were impeding the advance of his unit.

Sgt. Patterson single-handedly destroyed by rifle and grenade fire 5 enemy bunkers, killed 8 enemy soldiers, and captured 7 weapons. His dauntless courage and heroism inspired his platoon to resume the attack and to penetrate the enemy defensive position. Sgt. Patterson's action at the risk of his life has reflected great credit upon himself, his unit, and the U.S. Army.

Everett P. Pope
U.S. Marine Corps • WWII

"When speaking to young people, I often suggest to them that real courage is in doing the right thing. We all know what is right. We learn this at home, in church, and at school—but it frequently takes much courage to do what we know is right! I have tried to conduct my life by doing the right thing."

Rank and organization
Captain, U.S. Marine Corps, Company C,
1st Battalion, 1st Marines, 1st Marine Division.
Place and date
Peleliu Island, Palau group, 19-20 September 1944.

CITATION

For conspicuous gallantry and intrepidity at the risk of his life above and beyond the call of duty while serving as commanding officer of Company C, 1st Battalion, 1st Marines, 1st Marine Division, during action against enemy Japanese forces on Peleliu Island, Palau group, on 19-20 September 1944.

Subjected to pointblank cannon fire which caused heavy casualties and badly disorganized his company while assaulting a steep coral hill, Capt. Pope rallied his men and gallantly led them to the summit in the face of machinegun, mortar, and sniper fire. Forced by widespread hostile attack to deploy the remnants of his company thinly in order to hold the ground won, and with his machineguns out of order and insufficient water and ammunition, he remained on the exposed hill with 12 men and 1 wounded officer, determined to hold through the night.

Attacked continuously with grenades, machineguns, and rifles from 3 sides, he and his valiant men fiercely beat back or destroyed the enemy, resorting to hand-to-hand combat as the supply of ammunition dwindled, and still maintaining his lines with his 8 remaining riflemen when daylight brought more deadly fire and he was ordered to withdraw.

His valiant leadership against devastating odds while protecting the units below from heavy Japanese attack reflects the highest credit upon Capt. Pope and the U.S. Naval Service .

Alfred Rascon
U.S. Army • Vietnam

"The advice for life that I would offer is very simple: 'Treat others as you would want to be treated.' This is a restatement of the Golden Rule. Treat everyone with courtesy and with respect. Although we come from many different backgrounds, we must work together for the common good of the nation.

"When we look to people to respect, it shouldn't be because of their position or wealth. We need to be sure to acknowledge with respect those men and women who stay home and take care of their families...the teachers who teach and direct our children...those young soldiers, airmen, sailors, and marines who serve this nation. I am very fortunate and blessed. I came to this country as an immigrant, and I recognize how much I owe this nation."

Rank and organization
Specialist Fourth Class, U.S. Army, Reconnaissance Platoon,
Headquarters Company, 1st Battalion (Airborne),
503rd Infantry,173d Airborne Brigade (Separate)
Place and date
Republic of Vietnam, 16 March 1966.

CITATION

Specialist Four Alfred Rascon, distinguished himself by a series of extraordinarily courageous acts on 16 March 1966, while assigned as a medic to the Reconnaissance Platoon, Headquarters Company, 1st Battalion (Airborne), 503rd Infantry, 173d Airborne Brigade (Separate).

While moving to reinforce its sister battalion under intense enemy attack, the Reconnaissance Platoon came under heavy fire from a numerically superior enemy force. The intense enemy fire from crew-served weapons and grenades severely wounded several point squad soldiers. Specialist Rascon, ignoring directions to stay behind shelter until covering fire could be provided, made his way forward. He repeatedly tried to reach the severely wounded point machine-gunner laying on an open enemy trail but was driven back each time by the withering fire. Disregarding his personal safety, he jumped to his feet, ignoring flying bullets and exploding grenades to reach his comrade. To protect him from further wounds, he intentionally placed his body between the soldier and enemy machine guns, sustaining numerous shrapnel injuries and a serious wound to the hip. Disregarding his serious wounds, he dragged the larger soldier from the fire-raked trail.

Hearing the second machine-gunner yell that he was running out of ammunition, Specialist Rascon, under heavy enemy fire, crawled back to the wounded machine-gunner stripping him of his bandoleers of ammunition, giving them to the machine-gunner who continued his suppressive fire. Specialist Rascon fearing the abandoned machine gun with its ammunition and spare barrel could fall into enemy hands made his way to retrieve them. On the way, he was wounded in the face and torso by grenade fragments, but disregarded these wounds to recover the abandoned machine gun, ammunition and spare barrel items, enabling another soldier to provide added suppressive fire to the pinned-down squad.

In searching for the wounded, he saw the point grenadier being wounded by small arms fire and grenades being thrown at him. Disregarding his own life and his numerous wounds, Specialist Rascon reached and covered him with his body absorbing the blasts from the exploding grenades, and saving the soldier's life but sustaining additional wounds to his body. While making his way to the wounded point squad leader, grenades were hurled at the sergeant. Again, in complete disregard for his own life, he reached and covered the sergeant with his body, absorbing the full force of the grenade explosions. Once more Specialist Rascon was critically wounded by shrapnel but disregarded his own wounds to continue to search and aid the wounded.

Severely wounded, he remained on the battlefield, inspiring his fellow soldiers to continue the battle. After the enemy broke contact, he disregarded aid for himself, instead treating the wounded and directing their evacuation. Only after being placed on the evacuation helicopter did he allow aid to be given to him.

Specialist Rascon's extraordinary valor in the face of deadly enemy fire, his heroism in rescuing the wounded, and his gallantry by repeatedly risking his own life for his fellow soldiers are in keeping with the highest traditions of military service and reflect great credit upon himself, his unit, and the United States Army.

Congressional MOH Society

The Congressional Medal of Honor Society of the United States of America is perhaps the most exclusive organization in our country, and it is certainly one of the most unique. Its small membership includes men of all races, social classes, and economic levels. They range in stature from 5'2" to 6'5", in age from 48 to 90, and they live in all areas of our country. Among them are scholars and ordinary men, successful entrepreneurs and struggling laborers, ministers and misfits, rich and poor.

No amount of money, power, or influence can buy one's rite of passage to this exclusive circle, and unlike almost any other organization, this group's members hope that there will be no more inductees. Their purpose is:

- Creation of a bond of brotherhood and comradeship among all living recipients of the Medal of Honor.
- Maintaining the memory and respect for those who had died receiving the Medal of Honor, as well as those living recipients who had since died.
- Protection and preservation of the dignity and honor of the Medal of Honor at all times and on all occasions.
- Protecting the name of the Medal of Honor as well as individual Medal of Honor recipients from exploitation.
- Providing assistance and aid to needy Medal of Honor recipients, their spouses or widows, and their children.
- Promoting patriotism and allegiance to the government and constitution of the United States.
- To serve the United States in peace or war.
- To promote and perpetuate the principles upon which our nation is founded.
- To foster patriotism and inspire and stimulate our youth to become worthy citizens of our country.

Lieutenant Colonel Gordon R. Roberts
U.S. Army • Vietnam

"I have never been one who spends a lot of time talking or even listening to others talk about valor, patriotism, and service. As the old saying goes, 'Action speaks louder than words.' Thus, my advice for life, or creed would be: Take some time to look and see if what you have done or are doing matches up to what you are saying should be done. Spend your time setting the standard rather than talking about it."

Rank and organization
Sergeant (then Sp4c.), U.S. Army, Company B,
1st Battalion, 506th Infantry, 101st Airborne Division.
Place and date
Thua Thien Province, Republic of Vietnam, 11 July 1969.

CITATION
For conspicuous gallantry and intrepidity in action at the risk of his life above and beyond the call of duty. Sgt. Roberts distinguished himself while serving as a rifleman in Company B, during combat operations.

Sgt. Roberts' platoon was maneuvering along a ridge to attack heavily fortified enemy bunker positions which had pinned down an adjoining friendly company. As the platoon approached the enemy positions, it was suddenly pinned down by heavy automatic weapons and grenade fire from camouflaged enemy fortifications atop the overlooking hill. Seeing his platoon immobilized and in danger of failing in its mission, Sgt. Roberts crawled rapidly toward the closest enemy bunker. With complete disregard for his safety, he leaped to his feet and charged the bunker, firing as he ran. Despite the intense enemy fire directed at him, Sgt. Roberts silenced the 2-man bunker. Without hesitation, Sgt. Roberts continued his 1-man assault on a second bunker. As he neared the second bunker, a burst of enemy fire knocked his rifle from his hands. Sgt. Roberts picked up a rifle dropped by a comrade and continued his assault, silencing the bunker. He continued his charge against a third bunker and destroyed it with well-thrown hand grenades.

Although Sgt. Roberts was now cut off from his platoon, he continued his assault against a fourth enemy emplacement. He fought through a heavy hail of fire to join elements of the adjoining company which had been pinned down by the enemy fire. Although continually exposed to hostile fire, he assisted in moving wounded personnel from exposed positions on the hilltop to an evacuation area before returning to his unit.

By his gallant and selfless actions, Sgt. Roberts contributed directly to saving the lives of his comrades and served as an inspiration to his fellow soldiers in the defeat of the enemy force. Sgt. Roberts' extraordinary heroism in action at the risk of his life were in keeping with the highest traditions of the military service and reflect great credit upon himself, his unit, and the U.S. Army.

Chief Warrant Officer Louis R. Rocco
U.S. Army (Ret.) • Vietnam

"The following values are very dear to me: patriotism, courage (moral and physical), honesty, respect, compassion, and integrity. I believe that my word and my honor are the most important aspects of my life. My word is more important than wealth or power. To me, the powerful person is the individual that has many friends and who is a friend to others. My heroes have been the individuals who exhibited moral courage—those who stood up for what they thought was right and were willing to take any consequence for their actions—men who were honest, fair, compassionate, and competent. I feel saddened that these values are rarely taught today."

Rank and organization
Warrant Officer (then Sergeant First Class), U.S. Army,
Advisory Team 162, U.S. Military Assistance Command.
Place and date
Northeast of Katum, Republic of Vietnam, 24 May 1970.

CITATION

WO Rocco distinguished himself when he volunteered to accompany a medical evacuation team on an urgent mission to evacuate 8 critically wounded Army of the Republic of Vietnam
personnel.

As the helicopter approached the landing zone, it became the
target for intense enemy automatic weapons fire. Disregarding his
own safety, WO Rocco identified and placed accurate suppressive
fire on the enemy positions as the aircraft descended toward the
landing zone. Sustaining major damage from the enemy fire, the aircraft was forced to crash land, causing WO Rocco to sustain a fractured wrist and hip and a severely bruised back. Ignoring his
injuries, he extracted the survivors from the burning wreckage, sustaining burns to his own body. Despite intense enemy fire, WO
Rocco carried each unconscious man across approximately 20 meters of exposed terrain to the Army of the Republic of Vietnam
perimeter. On each trip, his severely burned hands and broken wrist
caused excruciating pain, but the lives of the unconscious crash survivors were more important than his personal discomfort, and he
continued his rescue efforts. Once inside the friendly position, WO
Rocco helped administer first aid to his wounded comrades until his
wounds and burns caused him to collapse and lose consciousness.

His bravery under fire and intense devotion to duty were directly responsible for saving 3 of his fellow soldiers from certain
death. His unparalleled bravery in the face of enemy fire, his complete disregard for his own pain and injuries, and his performance
were far above and beyond the call of duty and were in keeping with
the highest traditions of self-sacrifice and courage of the military
service.

Colonel Joseph C. Rodriguez
U.S. Army (Ret.) • Korea

"My advice for young men and women is: Life is short and precious; always make the effort to do good."

Rank and organization
Sergeant (then Pfc.), U.S. Army, Company F,
17th Infantry Regiment, 7th Infantry Division.
Place and date
Near Munye-ri, Korea, 21 May 1951.

CITATION

Sgt. Rodriguez, distinguished himself by conspicuous gallantry and intrepidity at the risk of his life above and beyond the call of duty in action against an armed enemy of the United Nations.

Sgt. Rodriguez, an assistant squad leader of the 2d Platoon, was participating in an attack against a fanatical hostile force occupying well-fortified positions on rugged commanding terrain, when his squad's advance was halted within approximately 60 yards by a withering barrage of automatic weapons and small-arms fire from 5 emplacements directly to the front and right and left flanks, to-gether with grenades which the enemy rolled down the hill toward the advancing troops. Fully aware of the odds against him, Sgt. Rodriguez leaped to his feet, dashed 60 yards up the fire-swept slope, and, after lobbing grenades into the first foxhole with deadly accuracy, ran around the left flank, silenced an automatic weapon with 2 grenades and continued his whirlwind assault to the top of the peak, wiping out 2 more foxholes and then, reaching the right flank, he tossed grenades into the remaining emplacement, de-stroying the gun and annihilating its crew.

Sgt. Rodriguez' intrepid actions exacted a toll of 15 enemy dead and, as a result of his incredible display of valor, the defense of the opposition was broken, the enemy routed, and the strategic strongpoint secured. His unflinching courage under fire and inspira-tional devotion to duty reflect highest credit on himself and uphold the honored traditions of the military service.

Sergeant First Class Ronald E. Rosser
U.S. Army (Ret.) • Korea

"As the oldest son of 17 children, I have had to accept responsibility for my actions and tried to be a role model for my brothers and sisters. I believe that one should serve and protect one's family, including the extended family.

"I have tried, throughout my life, to set a good example for children. If I was to offer advice about a creed or code of conduct for life, I would offer this: I have encouraged children to always be truthful, honest, and honorable. Our children will soon be the leaders of this nation."

Rank and organization
Corporal, U.S. Army, Heavy Mortar Company,
38th Infantry Regiment, 2d Infantry Division.
Place and date
Vicinity of Ponggilli, Korea, 12 January 1952.

CITATION

Cpl. Rosser, distinguished himself by conspicuous gallantry above and beyond the call of duty.

While assaulting heavily fortified enemy hill positions, Company L, 38th Infantry Regiment, was stopped by fierce automatic-weapons, small-arms, artillery, and mortar fire. Cpl. Rosser, a forward observer was with the lead platoon of Company L, when it came under fire from 2 directions. Cpl. Rosser turned his radio over to his assistant and, disregarding the enemy fire, charged the enemy positions armed with only carbine and a grenade. At the first bunker, he silenced its occupants with a burst from his weapon. Gaining the top of the hill, he killed 2 enemy soldiers, and then went down the trench, killing 5 more as he advanced. He then hurled his grenade into a bunker and shot 2 other soldiers as they emerged.

Having exhausted his ammunition, he returned through the enemy fire to obtain more ammunition and grenades and charged the hill once more. Calling on others to follow him, he assaulted 2 more enemy bunkers. Although those who attempted to join him became casualties, Cpl. Rosser once again exhausted his ammunition, obtained a new supply, and returned to the hilltop a third time, and hurled grenades into the enemy positions. During this heroic action Cpl. Rosser single-handedly killed at least 13 of the enemy. After exhausting his ammunition, he accompanied the withdrawing platoon, and though himself wounded, made several trips across open terrain still under enemy fire to help remove other men injured more seriously than himself.

This outstanding soldier's courageous and selfless devotion to duty is worthy of emulation by all men. He has contributed magnificently to the high traditions of the military service.

Master Sergeant Donald Rudolph
U.S. Army (Ret.) • WWII

"If I was to offer my creed or code of conduct for life, I would give this advice: 'Never ask someone to do something that you are not willing to do yourself.'"

Rank and organization
Second Lieutenant, U.S. Army, Company E,
20th Infantry, 6th Infantry Division.
Place and date
Munoz, Luzon, Philippine Islands, 5 February 1945.

CITATION

2d Lt. Rudolph (then T/Sgt.) was acting as platoon leader at Munoz, Luzon, Philippine Islands. While administering first aid on the battlefield, he observed enemy fire issuing from a nearby culvert. Crawling to the culvert with rifle and grenades, he killed 3 of the enemy concealed there. He then worked his way across open terrain toward a line of enemy pillboxes which had immobilized his company. Nearing the first pillbox, he hurled a grenade through its embrasure and charged the position. With his bare hands he tore away the wood and tin covering, then dropped a grenade through the opening, killing the enemy gunners and destroying their machinegun.

Ordering several riflemen to cover his further advance, 2d Lt. Rudolph seized a pick mattock and made his way to the second pillbox. Piercing its top with the mattock, he dropped a grenade through the hole, fired several rounds from his rifle into it and smothered any surviving enemy by sealing the hole and the embrasure with earth. In quick succession, he attacked and neutralized 6 more pillboxes.

Later, when his platoon was attacked by an enemy tank, he advanced under covering fire, climbed to the top of the tank, and dropped a white phosphorus grenade through the turret, destroying the crew.

Through his outstanding heroism, superb courage, and leadership, and complete disregard for his own safety, 2d Lt. Rudolph cleared a path for an advance, which culminated in one of the most decisive victories of the Philippine campaign.

George T. Sakato
U.S. Army • WWII

"Make sure you finish school and, if possible, continue your education. I would ask every one of you to consider service to our nation. The discipline you learn will allow you to take and give orders. Discipline is an important part of life. I would also ask that you respect the flag because freedom came at great expense. Always do what is right because moral courage is as important as physical courage. And finally, serve God and country, both before self."

CITATION

Private George T. Sakato distinguished himself by extraordinary heroism in action on 29 October 1944, on hill 617 in the vicinity of Biffontaine, France.

After his platoon had virtually destroyed two enemy defense lines, during which he personally killed five enemy soldiers and captured four, his unit was pinned down by heavy enemy fire. Disregarding the enemy fire, Private Sakato made a one-man rush that encouraged his platoon to charge and destroy the enemy strongpoint.

While his platoon was reorganizing, he proved to be the inspiration of his squad in halting a counter-attack on the left flank during which his squad leader was killed. Taking charge of the squad, he continued his relentless tactics, using an enemy rifle and P-38 pistol to stop an organized enemy attack. During this entire action, he killed 12 and wounded two, personally captured four, and assisted his platoon in taking 34 prisoners. By continuously ignoring enemy fire, and by his gallant courage and fighting spirit, he turned impending defeat into victory and helped his platoon complete its mission.

Private Sakato's extraordinary heroism and devotion to duty are in keeping with the highest traditions of military service and reflect great credit on him, his unit, and the United States Army.

Clarence Sasser
U.S. Army • Vietnam

"I usually tell kids to look out for themselves. You can do that by making sure that everything you do is wise and to your best benefit. Always think, always question, 'Is this the wise thing to do? Is it to my benefit?' If the answer is no, then don't do it. Your choices make your life. Bad choices mean a bad life, a life that will not be to your benefit. Wise choices, good choices mean a good life. Think about it!"

Rank and organization
Specialist Fifth Class (then Pfc.), U.S. Army, Headquarters
Company, 3d Battalion, 60th Infantry, 9th Infantry Division.
Place and date
Ding Tuong Province, Republic of Vietnam, 10 January 1968.

CITATION

For conspicuous gallantry and intrepidity in action at the risk of his life above and beyond the call of duty. Sp5c. Sasser distinguished himself while assigned to Headquarters and Headquarters Company, 3d Battalion.

He was serving as a medical aidman with Company A, 3d Battalion, on a reconnaissance in force operation. His company was making an air assault when suddenly it was taken under heavy small arms, recoilless rifle, machinegun, and rocket fire from well fortified enemy positions on 3 sides of the landing zone. During the first few minutes, over 30 casualties were sustained. Without hesitation, Sp5c. Sasser ran across an open rice paddy through a hail of fire to assist the wounded. After helping 1 man to safety, he was painfully wounded in the left shoulder by fragments of an exploding rocket. Refusing medical attention, he ran through a barrage of rocket and automatic weapons fire to aid casualties of the initial attack and, after giving them urgently needed treatment, continued to search for other wounded.

Despite 2 additional wounds immobilizing his legs, he dragged himself through the mud toward another soldier 100 meters away. Although in agonizing pain and faint from loss of blood, Sp5c. Sasser reached the man, treated him, and proceeded on to encourage another group of soldiers to crawl 200 meters to relative safety. There he attended their wounds for 5 hours until they were evacuated.

Sp5c. Sasser's extraordinary heroism is in keeping with the highest traditions of the military service and reflects great credit upon himself, his unit, and the U.S. Army.

Colonel Edward R. Schowalter, Jr.
U.S. Army (Ret.) • Korea

"I will no longer talk of war. My creed has been 'God and Country.' Although at times I've failed miserably to live up to this creed, I have tried. The only time I make an exception to my silence is when I'm asked to speak in honor of those who gave their lives in war."

Rank and organization
First Lieutenant, U.S. Army, Company A,
31st Infantry Regiment, 7th Infantry Division.
Place and date
Near Kumhwa, Korea, 14 October 1952.

CITATION

1st Lt. Schowalter, commanding Company A, distinguished himself by conspicuous gallantry and indomitable courage above and beyond the call of duty in action against the enemy.

Committed to attack and occupy a key-approach to the primary objective, the 1st Platoon of his company came under heavy vicious small-arms, grenade, and mortar fire within 50 yards of the enemy-held strongpoint, halting the advance and inflicting several casualties. The 2d Platoon moved up in support at this juncture, and although wounded, 1st Lt. Schowalter continued to spearhead the assault.

Nearing the objective he was severely wounded by a grenade fragment but, refusing medical aid, he led his men into the trenches and began routing the enemy from the bunkers with grenades. Suddenly, from a burst of fire from a hidden cove off the trench, he was again wounded. Although suffering from his wounds, he refused to relinquish command and continued issuing orders and encouraging his men until the commanding ground was secured, and then he was evacuated.

1st Lt. Schowalter's unflinching courage, extraordinary heroism, and inspirational leadership reflect the highest credit upon himself and are in keeping with the highest traditions of the military service.

Colonel Carl Sitter
U.S. Marine Corps (Ret.) • Korea

"A leader must embody qualities which include simplicity, judgment, justice, enthusiasm, perseverance, tact, courage, faith, loyalty, truthfulness, and honor. These may be called the 'building blocks of leadership.' The extent to which they are ingredients in your character and personality determines your value as a leader. There are two types of courage: physical and moral courage. The former is by far the more common of the two. Moral courage sustains men in mental crisis because it gives a man the courage of his convictions.

"I served for more than thirty years in the United States Marine Corps and then worked and eventually retired from the Virginia Department of Social Services. In 1998, at the age of seventy-five, I went back to school to become a minister. I went back to school to learn more about the Lord and to use that knowledge to help all people. God told us to love everyone."

Rank and organization
Captain, U.S. Marine Corps, Company G, 3d Battalion,
1st Marines, 1st Marine Division (Rein.).
Place and date
Hagaru-ri, Korea, 29 and 30 November 1950.

CITATION

For conspicuous gallantry and intrepidity at the risk of his life above and beyond the call of duty as commanding officer of Company G, in action against enemy aggressor forces. Ordered to break through enemy-infested territory to reinforce his battalion the morning of 29 November, Capt. Sitter continuously exposed himself to enemy fire as he led his company forward and, despite 25 percent casualties suffered in the furious action, succeeded in driving through to his objective. Assuming the responsibility of attempting to seize and occupy a strategic area occupied by a hostile force of regiment strength deeply entrenched on a snow-covered hill commanding the entire valley southeast of the town, as well as the line of march of friendly troops withdrawing to the south, he reorganized his depleted units the following morning and boldly led them up the steep, frozen hillside under blistering fire, encouraging and redeploying his troops as casualties occurred and directing forward platoons as they continued the drive to the top of the ridge.

During the night when a vastly outnumbering enemy launched a sudden, vicious counterattack, setting the hill ablaze with mortar, machine gun, and automatic-weapons fire and taking a heavy toll in troops, Capt. Sitter visited each foxhole and gun position, coolly deploying and integrating reinforcing units consisting of service personnel unfamiliar with infantry tactics into a coordinated combat team and instilling in every man the will and determination to hold his position at all costs. With the enemy penetrating his lines in repeated counterattacks which often required hand-to-hand combat, and, on one occasion infiltrating to the command post with handgrenades, he fought gallantly with his men in repulsing and killing the fanatic attackers in each encounter. Painfully wounded in the face, arms, and chest by bursting grenades, he staunchly refused to be evacuated and continued to fight on until a successful defense of the area was assured with a loss to the enemy of more than 50 percent dead, wounded, and captured.

His valiant leadership, superb tactics, and great personal valor throughout 36 hours of bitter combat reflect the highest credit upon Capt. Sitter and the U.S. Naval Service.

Richard K. Sorenson
U.S. Marine Corps • WWII

"We must dedicate ourselves to the principle that 'freedom under God' is man's destiny. We must not only live our lives according to this principle, but also defend it unto death with the courage of free men. Our country won its freedom in one generation, but in one generation it could also lose it."

Rank and organization
Private, U.S. Marine Corps Reserve, 4th Marine Division.
Place and date
Namur Island, Kwajalein Atoll Marshall Islands,
1-2 February 1944.

CITATION

For conspicuous gallantry and intrepidity at the risk of his life above and beyond the call of duty while serving with an assault battalion attached to the 4th Marine Division during the battle of Namur Island, Kwajalein Atoll, Marshall Islands, on 1-2 February 1944.

Putting up a brave defense against a particularly violent counterattack by the enemy during invasion operations, Pvt. Sorenson and 5 other marines occupying a shellhole were endangered by a Japanese grenade thrown into their midst. Unhesitatingly, and with complete disregard for his own safety, Pvt. Sorenson hurled himself upon the deadly weapon, heroically taking the full impact of the explosion. As a result of his gallant action, he was severely wounded, but the lives of his comrades were saved.

His great personal valor and exceptional spirit of self-sacrifice in the face of almost certain death were in keeping with the highest traditions of the U.S. Naval Service.

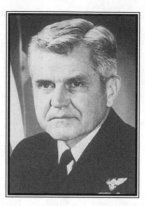

Vice Admiral James B. Stockdale
U.S. Navy (Ret.) • Vietnam

"One's integrity can give a person something to rely on when perspectives seem to blur, when rules and principles seem to waver, and when faced with a hard choice of right and wrong. A clear conscience is one's only protection."

Rank and organization
Rear Admiral (then Captain), U.S. Navy.
Place and date
Hoa Lo prison, Hanoi, North Vietnam, 4 September 1969.

CITATION

For conspicuous gallantry and intrepidity at the risk of his life above and beyond the call of duty while senior naval officer in the Prisoner of War camps of North Vietnam.

Recognized by his captors as the leader in the Prisoners of War resistance to interrogation and in their refusal to participate in propaganda exploitation, Rear Adm. Stockdale was singled out for interrogation and attendant torture after he was detected in a covert communications attempt. Sensing the start of another purge, and aware that his earlier efforts at self-disfiguration to dissuade his captors from exploiting him for propaganda purposes had resulted in cruel and agonizing punishment, Rear Adm. Stockdale resolved to make himself a symbol of resistance regardless of personal sacrifice. He deliberately inflicted a near-mortal wound to his person in order to convince his captors of his willingness to give up his life rather than capitulate. He was subsequently discovered and revived by the North Vietnamese who, convinced of his indomitable spirit, abated in their employment of excessive harassment and torture toward all of the Prisoners of War.

By his heroic action, at great peril to himself, he earned the everlasting gratitude of his fellow prisoners and of his country. Rear Adm. Stockdale's valiant leadership and extraordinary courage in a hostile environment sustain and enhance the finest traditions of the U.S. Naval Service.

Colonel James L. Stone
U.S. Army (Ret.) • Korea

"We should be forever grateful that we are citizens of the greatest nation on earth; no other country can provide you with the world's highest living standard, and the many freedoms that all of us enjoy in our daily lives.

"Perhaps, sometime in your life, you be might be asked to serve your nation, or serve in the Armed Forces of the United States. Please do not hesitate—serve with pride, dignity, and honor."

Rank and organization
First Lieutenant, U.S. Army, Company E,
8th Cavalry Regiment, 1st Cavalry Division.
Place and date
Near Sokkogae, Korea, 21 and 22 November 1951.

CITATION

1st Lt. Stone, distinguished himself by conspicuous gallantry and indomitable courage above and beyond the call of duty in action against the enemy.

When his platoon, holding a vital outpost position, was attacked by overwhelming Chinese forces, 1st Lt. Stone stood erect and exposed to the terrific enemy fire calmly directed his men in the defense. A defensive flame-thrower failing to function, he personally moved to its location, further exposing himself, and personally repaired the weapon. Throughout a second attack, 1st Lt. Stone, though painfully wounded, personally carried the only remaining light machine gun from place to place in the position in order to bring fire upon the Chinese advancing from 2 directions.

Throughout, he continued to encourage and direct his depleted platoon in its hopeless defense. Although again wounded, he continued the fight with his carbine, still exposing himself as an example to his men. When this final overwhelming assault swept over the platoon's position, his voice could still be heard faintly urging his men to carry on, until he lost consciousness. Only because of this officer's driving spirit and heroic action was the platoon emboldened to make its brave but hopeless last ditch stand.

Sergeant Major Kenneth E. Stumpf
U.S. Army (Ret.) • Vietnam

"Always give your highest honor and respect to your mother.

"Sometimes it's best to say nothing at all.

"To lose is temporary—to give up is forever. Always channel your energy into positive things. You control your destiny—set goals and work to achieve them. The best thing you can learn from a mistake is not to repeat it.

"Always maintain a high level of honesty, dedication, and discipline. Be all you can be.

"Find someone who displays a positive influence on your life.

"You know right from wrong; be accountable for all your actions.

"You live in a free country. Thank a war veteran."

Rank and organization
Staff Sergeant (then Sp4c.), U.S. Army, Company C,
1st Battalion, 35th Infantry, 25th Infantry Division.
Place and date
Near Duc Pho, Republic of Vietnam, 25 April 1967.

CITATION

For conspicuous gallantry and intrepidity in action at the risk of his life above and beyond the call of duty. S/Sgt. Stumpf distinguished himself while serving as a squad leader of the 3d Platoon, Company C, on a search and destroy mission.

As S/Sgt. Stumpf's company approached a village, it encountered a North Vietnamese rifle company occupying a well-fortified bunker complex. During the initial contact, 3 men from his squad fell wounded in front of a hostile machinegun emplacement. The enemy's heavy volume of fire prevented the unit from moving to the aid of the injured men, but S/Sgt. Stumpf left his secure position in a deep trench and ran through the barrage of incoming rounds to reach his wounded comrades. He picked up 1 of the men and carried him back to the safety of the trench. Twice more S/Sgt. Stumpf dashed forward while the enemy turned automatic weapons and machineguns upon him, yet he managed to rescue the remaining 2 wounded squad members.

He then organized his squad and led an assault against several enemy bunkers from which continuously heavy fire was being received. He and his squad successfully eliminated 2 of the bunker positions, but one to the front of the advancing platoon remained a serious threat. Arming himself with extra hand grenades, S/Sgt. Stumpf ran over open ground, through a volley of fire directed at him by a determined enemy, toward the machinegun position. As he reached the bunker, he threw a hand grenade through the aperture. It was immediately returned by the occupants, forcing S/Sgt. Stumpf to take cover. Undaunted, he pulled the pins on 2 more grenades, held them for a few seconds after activation, then hurled them into the position, this time successfully destroying the emplacement. With the elimination of this key position, his unit was able to assault and overrun the enemy.

S/Sgt. Stumpf's relentless spirit of aggressiveness, intrepidity, and ultimate concern for the lives of his men, are in the highest traditions of the military service and reflect great credit upon himself and the U.S. Army.

Colonel James E. Swett
U.S. Marine Corps (Ret.) • WWII

"My parents spent a great deal of time correcting, directing, and just plain straightening me out. I loved them dearly. They were always honest with me, and I was always honest with them. I believe the motto for our family was and is, 'God is with you: He is always there.' I know the Lord Jesus Christ was in the plane with me every time I climbed into my cockpit. I would offer this advice: Always do what is right, never give up, and always be honest."

Rank and organization
First Lieutenant, U.S. Marine Corps Reserve,
Marine Fighter Squadron 221, with Marine Aircraft Group 12,
1st Marine Aircraft Wing.
Place and date
Solomon Islands area, 7 April 1943.
Other Navy award
Distinguished Flying Cross with 1 Gold Star.

CITATION

For extraordinary heroism and personal valor above and beyond the call of duty, as division leader of Marine Fighting Squadron 221 with Marine Aircraft Group 12, 1st Marine Aircraft Wing, in action against enemy Japanese aerial forces in the Solomons Islands area, 7 April 1943.

In a daring flight to intercept a wave of 150 Japanese planes, 1st Lt. Swett unhesitatingly hurled his 4-plane division into action against a formation of 15 enemy bombers and personally exploded 3 hostile planes in midair with accurate and deadly fire during his dive. Although separated from his division while clearing the heavy concentration of antiaircraft fire, he boldly attacked 6 enemy bombers, engaged the first 4 in turn and, unaided, shot down all in flames. Exhausting his ammunition as he closed the fifth Japanese bomber, he relentlessly drove his attack against terrific opposition which partially disabled his engine, shattered the windscreen, and slashed his face. In spite of this, he brought his battered plane down with skillful precision in the water off Tulagi without further injury.

The superb airmanship and tenacious fighting spirit which enabled 1st Lt. Swett to destroy 7 enemy bombers in a single flight were in keeping with the highest traditions of the U.S. Naval Service.

Major James A. Taylor
U.S. Army (Ret.) • Vietnam

"There is no substitute for integrity. Your word is your 'Badge of Honor.' Assert yourself, take action, seek success. Education and self-discipline are key elements to succeed in life; however, you will not succeed (in life) without the desire to do so.

"I would also like to offer the following advice to young men and women. It is the advice given to me by my father, the advice which has helped me overcome many of life challenges: You will encounter many high and low points throughout your lifetime and hundreds of obstacles, but don't be afraid to make or admit a mistake. Turn a negative into a positive and never say you can't do something. Think about what you have done, right or wrong, improve or correct it, and move on to the next challenge. Through positive thinking, hard work, dedication, and sacrifice, you can succeed."

Rank and organization
Captain (then 1st Lt.), U.S. Army, Troop B,
1st Cavalry, Americal Division.
Place and date
West of Que Son, Republic of Vietnam, 9 November 1967.

CITATION

Capt. Taylor, Armor, was serving as executive officer of Troop B, 1st Squadron. His troop was engaged in an attack on a fortified position west of Que Son when it came under intense enemy recoilless rifle, mortar, and automatic weapons fire from an enemy strong point located immediately to its front. One armored cavalry assault vehicle was hit immediately by recoilless rifle fire and all 5 crewmembers were wounded. Aware that the stricken vehicle was in grave danger of exploding, Capt. Taylor rushed forward and personally extracted the wounded to safety despite the hail of enemy fire and exploding ammunition.

Within minutes, a second armored cavalry assault vehicle was hit by multiple recoilless rifle rounds. Despite the continuing intense enemy fire, Capt. Taylor moved forward on foot to rescue the wounded men from the burning vehicle and personally removed all the crewmen to the safety of a nearby dike. Moments later the vehicle exploded. As he was returning to his vehicle, a bursting mortar round painfully wounded Capt. Taylor, yet he valiantly returned to his vehicle to relocate the medical evacuation landing zone to an area closer to the front lines.

As he was moving his vehicle, it came under machinegun fire from an enemy position not 50 yards away. Capt. Taylor engaged the position with his machinegun, killing the 3-man crew. Upon arrival at the new evacuation site, still another vehicle was struck. Once again Capt. Taylor rushed forward and pulled the wounded from the vehicle, loaded them aboard his vehicle, and returned them safely to the evacuation site.

His actions of unsurpassed valor were a source of inspiration to his entire troop, contributed significantly to the success of the overall assault on the enemy position, and were directly responsible for saving the lives of a number of his fellow soldiers. His actions were in keeping with the highest traditions of the military profession and reflect great credit upon himself, his unit, and the U.S. Army.

Brian M. Thacker
U.S. Army • Vietnam

"I am often asked, 'What did you think about, and what gave you the most comfort during the eight days that you were alone and surrounded by the enemy, knowing they were continually searching to find you?' My answer might sound a little odd because I am not really a 'church person,' but the three things that gave me the most comfort were the Lord's Prayer, the 23rd Psalm, and the first few lines from the poem *Invictus*.

"The advice I would offer to young men and women is this: Moral courage is as important as physical courage. Without courage, all other virtues are difficult, if not impossible, to live up to."

Rank and organization
First Lieutenant, U.S. Army, Battery A,
1st Battalion, 92d Artillery.
Place and date
Kontum Province, Republic of Vietnam, 31 March 1971.

CITATION

For conspicuous gallantry and intrepidity in action at the risk of his life above and beyond the call of duty. 1st Lt. Thacker, Field Artillery, Battery A, distinguished himself while serving as the team leader of an Integrated Observation System collocated with elements of 2 Army of the Republic of Vietnam units at Fire Base 6.

A numerically superior North Vietnamese Army force launched a well-planned, dawn attack on the small, isolated, hilltop fire base. Employing rockets, grenades, flame-throwers, and automatic weapons, the enemy forces penetrated the perimeter defenses and engaged the defenders in hand-to-hand combat. Throughout the morning and early afternoon, 1st Lt. Thacker rallied and encouraged the U.S. and Republic of Vietnam soldiers in heroic efforts to repulse the enemy.

He occupied a dangerously exposed observation position for a period of 4 hours while directing friendly air strikes and artillery fire against the assaulting enemy forces. His personal bravery and inspired leadership enabled the outnumbered friendly forces to inflict a maximum of casualties on the attacking enemy forces and prevented the base from being overrun.

By late afternoon, the situation had become untenable. 1st Lt. Thacker organized and directed the withdrawal of the remaining friendly forces. With complete disregard for his personal safety, he remained inside the perimeter alone to provide covering fire with his M-16 rifle until all other friendly forces had escaped from the besieged fire base. Then, in an act of supreme courage, he called for friendly artillery fire on his own position to allow his comrades more time to withdraw safely from the area and, at the same time, inflict even greater casualties on the enemy forces. Although wounded and unable to escape from the area himself, he successfully eluded the enemy forces for 8 days until friendly forces regained control of the fire base.

The extraordinary courage and selflessness displayed by 1st Lt. Thacker were an inspiration to his comrades and are in the highest traditions of the military service.

Colonel Leo K. Thorsness
U.S. Air Force (Ret.) • Vietnam

"While a POW in Hanoi for six years, I put into conscious thinking a 'plan for life.' My formula is very basic. It is this: Life = Goals + Commitments + Plans. My definition of life is: living a full, productive Christian life.

"GOALS: Goals take a lot of cerebration—a lot of deep thinking. I'm talking about two or three major goals in life. For most, that includes the spiritual life. Also, most will include family, security, and success. Success, unfortunately, is often measured in dollars instead of integrity.

"COMMITMENTS: These are the hardest as they must come from the heart and are life changing. A simple example is a goal to be healthy. In essence, that requires exercising more and eating less and better—a struggle every day for many people. Likewise, a commitment to live as Christ wants us to live is a major change for the majority of us. Commitments are hard.

"PLANS: Plans are the easy part. If you keep your commitments, the plans fall into place.

"For much of my time as a POW and in my years since release from Hanoi in 1973, this simple formula has served me well."

Rank and organization
Lieutenant Colonel (then Maj.), U.S. Air Force,
357th Tactical Fighter Squadron.
Place and date
Over North Vietnam, 19 April 1967.

CITATION

For conspicuous gallantry and intrepidity in action at the risk of his life above and beyond the call of duty. As pilot of an F-105 aircraft, Lt. Col. Thorsness was on a surface-to-air missile suppression mission over North Vietnam. Lt. Col. Thorsness and his wingman attacked and silenced a surface-to-air missile site with air-to-ground missiles, and then destroyed a second surface-to-air missile site with bombs. In the attack on the second missile site, Lt. Col. Thorsness' wingman was shot down by intensive antiaircraft fire, and the 2 crewmembers abandoned their aircraft. Lt. Col. Thorsness circled the descending parachutes to keep the crewmembers in sight and relay their position to the Search and Rescue Center.

During this maneuver, a MIG-17 was sighted in the area. Lt. Col. Thorsness immediately initiated an attack and destroyed the MIG. Because his aircraft was low on fuel, he was forced to depart the area in search of a tanker. Upon being advised that 2 helicopters were orbiting over the downed crew's position and that there were hostile MIGs in the area posing a serious threat to the helicopters, Lt. Col. Thorsness, despite his low fuel condition, decided to return alone through a hostile environment of surface-to-air missile and antiaircraft defenses to the downed crew's position.

As he approached the area, he spotted 4 MIG-17 aircraft and immediately initiated an attack on the MIGs, damaging 1 and driving the others away from the rescue scene. When it became apparent that an aircraft in the area was critically low on fuel and the crew would have to abandon the aircraft unless they could reach a tanker, Lt. Col. Thorsness, although critically short on fuel himself, helped to avert further possible loss of life and a friendly aircraft by recovering at a forward operating base, thus allowing the aircraft in emergency fuel condition to refuel safely.

Lt. Col. Thorsness' extraordinary heroism, self-sacrifice, and personal bravery involving conspicuous risk of life were in the highest traditions of the military service, and have reflected great credit upon himself and the U.S. Air Force.

PEOPLE OR TRUCKS

I taxied with two F-105s fighters to the end of the runway at Takhli, Thailand, in January 1967. I had about 50 Wild Weasel missions over North Vietnam in my assigned mission to seek out and destroy Surface to Air Missile (SAM) sites.

We had the standard wait at the end of the runway while the ground crews armed our guns, bombs, and air-to-ground missiles. The wait was especially long as several aircraft were landing. As we waited to take the runway, my backseater and I talked about the Thai peasants who were working at the end of the runway. It seemed the women were doing most of the work while the men were hunkering and smoking cigarettes. We couldn't hear the conversation, of course, but it was obvious that none were working too hard and were having a good time as they laughed, pointed, and exchanged lots of banter. Harry, my backseater, and I commented that it was nice they were enjoying life.

Normally all North Vietnamese SAMs were kept within a hundred miles of Hanoi or so. Occasionally they would sneak one down by the DMZ to get a shot at a B-52 or refueling tanker. There were overnight reports from electronic intelligence aircraft that the North Vietnamese may have sneaked a SAM just north of the DMZ. Our early morning mission was to see if it was there and destroy it.

My wingman and I made the 40 minute flight to the southern part of North Vietnam. We crisscrossed several times the narrow span of North Vietnam between Laos and the Gulf of Tonkin without picking up any electric signals of the SAM's radar.

We stayed at least 10,000 feet above a low, solid cloud cover so if they quickly launched a SAM, we would have time to see and outmaneuver it. We saw no SAMs and heard no signals and were getting close to our low fuel depart time. Just then, faster than I'd seen, the solid but thin, low cloud layer quickly burned off from the early morning sun. I dropped down to about 5,000 feet for a better visual inspection of the suspected SAM site. What I saw instead were hundreds of North Vietnamese working to repair the previous day's bomb damage to Highway 1, the North Vietnamese main route for supplies from Hanoi to the South. The workers were out in the open; a perfect target for my CBU bombs. CBUs are mother bombs that, when dropped, have a shell that opens and about a thousand hand grenade sized bomblets spew out and explode when hitting the ground. CBUs are perfect weapons for thin-skinned things like missiles and people.

It was nearly time to head home and we found a perfectly legitimate target—North Vietnamese helping get supplies to their troops in South Vietnam to fight and kill Americans. I looked over the area and about a mile north of the peasants were several trucks and busses—obviously transport for the workers.

I made a radio call, "Cadillac two, afterburner NOW; go bomb mode." I pulled my nose up and climbed for 18,000 feet to roll on a bomb run. In the few seconds it took to climb, my wingman called, "Cadillac lead, what's the target?"

We had two legitimate targets—people or trucks—and we had the right weapons for either. While reaching for 18,000 feet, the image of happy Thai workers we had watched just an hour ago flashed in my mind. Here were similar people, living under communism, forced to work in an open area filling bomb craters and fearing they were about to be bombed. My mind said the best target was the peasants; my heart said it was the trucks. The Thai peasants image stayed in my mind. The entire thought process lasted the few seconds I had before deciding the target: people or trucks.

As vividly as if it were yesterday, I recall turning my head and looking at my left shoulder. There sat Jesus Christ. I asked, "People or trucks?" As quickly as I asked, He answered, "Trucks."

As we rolled over inverted and started pulling our nose earthward into a bomb run, I called, "Cadillac two, we hit the trucks!"

—*Leo Thorsness*

Colonel John J. Tomanic
U.S. Army (Ret.) • WWII

"I grew up in an economically depressed neighborhood comprised of immigrant families from many different ethnic backgrounds. The value of a strong work ethic was always demonstrated. I learned the importance of self-reliance and the intense desire and will required to succeed. These characteristics, plus determination, insured success.

"If I was to recommend a code of conduct for life, I would address these qualities. There is no doubt in my mind that the characteristics nurtured during my youth of a strong work ethic, self-reliance, and the intense desire and will to succeed, coupled with the determination to accept any assigned task, significantly influenced my life.

"These traits were indispensable to my ability to survive and succeed on the battlefields of Europe during WWII."

———•◦•———

Rank and organization
First Lieutenant, U.S. Army, Company I,
15th Infantry, 3d Infantry Division.
Place and date
Saulx de Vesoul, France, 12 September 1944.

CITATION

For conspicuous gallantry and intrepidity at risk of life above and beyond the call of duty on 12 September 1944, in an attack on Saulx de Vesoul, France, 1st Lt. Tominac charged alone over 50 yards of exposed terrain onto an enemy roadblock to dispatch a 3-man crew of German machine gunners with a single burst from his Thompson machinegun. After smashing the enemy outpost, he led 1 of his squads in the annihilation of a second hostile group defended by mortar, machinegun automatic pistol, rifle, and grenade fire, killing about 30 of the enemy.

Reaching the suburbs of the town, he advanced 50 yards ahead of his men to reconnoiter a third enemy position which commanded the road with a 77-mm. SP gun supported by infantry elements. The SP gun opened fire on his supporting tank, setting it afire with a direct hit. A fragment from the same shell painfully wounded 1st Lt. Tominac in the shoulder, knocking him to the ground. As the crew abandoned the M-4 tank, which was rolling down hill toward the enemy, 1st Lt. Tominac picked himself up and jumped onto the hull of the burning vehicle.

Despite withering enemy machinegun, mortar, pistol, and sniper fire, which was ricocheting off the hull and turret of the M-4, 1st Lt. Tominac climbed to the turret and gripped the 50-caliber antiaircraft machinegun. Plainly silhouetted against the sky, painfully wounded, and with the tank burning beneath his feet, he directed bursts of machinegun fire on the roadblock, the SP gun, and the supporting German infantrymen, and forced the enemy to withdraw from his prepared position. Jumping off the tank before it exploded, 1st Lt. Tominac refused evacuation despite his painful wound. Calling upon a sergeant to extract the shell fragments from his shoulder with a pocketknife, he continued to direct the assault, led his squad in a hand grenade attack against a fortified position occupied by 32 of the enemy armed with machineguns, machine pistols, and rifles, and compelled them to surrender.

His outstanding heroism and exemplary leadership resulted in the destruction of 4 successive enemy defensive positions, surrender of a vital sector of the city Saulx de Vesoul, and the death or capture of at least 60 of the enemy.

Colonel Jay R. Vargas
U.S. Marine Corps (Ret.) • Vietnam

"I believe no one can be a leader unless he:
1. Believes in God.
2. Always sets the example as a leader and keeps the standards high!
3. Is the type of leader who will never ask anyone to do anything he wouldn't do himself—whether it be in combat or peacetime.
4. Takes care of his troops before himself!
5. Can be patient and not afraid to be humble. If one must brag about himself, then do it in front of the mirror each morning.
6. Puts integrity as his #1 leadership tool when leading his command.
7. Lastly, he must never be afraid to say he made a mistake!"

Rank and organization
Major (then Capt.), U.S. Marine Corps, Company G,
2d Battalion, 4th Marines, 9th Marine Amphibious Brigade.
Place and date
Dai Do, Republic of Vietnam, 30 April to 2 May 1968.

CITATION

For conspicuous gallantry and intrepidity at the risk of his life above and beyond the call of duty while serving as commanding officer, Company G, in action against enemy forces from 30 April to 2 May 1968. On 1 May 1968, though suffering from wounds he had incurred while relocating his unit under heavy enemy fire the preceding day, Maj. Vargas combined Company G with two other companies and led his men in an attack on the fortified village of Dai Do. Exercising expert leadership, he maneuvered his marines across 700 meters of open rice paddy while under intense enemy mortar, rocket and artillery fire and obtained a foothold in 2 hedgerows on the enemy perimeter, only to have elements of his company become pinned down by the intense enemy fire. Leading his reserve platoon to the aid of his beleaguered men, Maj. Vargas inspired his men to renew their relentless advance, while destroying a number of enemy bunkers.

Again wounded by grenade fragments, he refused aid as he moved about the hazardous area reorganizing his unit into a strong defense perimeter at the edge of the village. Shortly after the objective was secured, the enemy commenced a series of counterattacks and probes which lasted throughout the night but were unsuccessful as the gallant defenders of Company G stood firm in their hard-won enclave.

Reinforced the following morning, the marines launched a renewed assault through Dai Do on the village of Dinh To, to which the enemy retaliated with a massive counterattack resulting in hand-to-hand combat. Maj. Vargas remained in the open, encouraging and rendering assistance to his marines when he was hit for the third time in the 3-day battle. Observing his battalion commander sustain a serious wound, he disregarded his excruciating pain, crossed the fire-swept area and carried his commander to a covered position, then resumed supervising and encouraging his men while simultaneously assisting in organizing the battalion's perimeter defense.

His gallant actions uphold the highest traditions of the Marine Corps and the U.S. Naval Service.

Major George E. Wahlen
U.S. Army (Ret.) • WWII
*(Received the Medal of Honor as a Navy
Corpsman with the U.S. Marine Corps.*

"Before I experienced combat, I was never very religious. I was worried that I would not be able to do what was required of me so I began to pray for God to give me the courage to do the right thing while I was trying to take care of my Marines. Even though I was afraid of dying, I was more afraid of not doing the best or what was right for the men in my care. I was never concerned about medals, I just wanted to do the right thing. I wanted my conscience to be clear. If you always do what's right, you will have peace."

Rank and organization
Pharmacist's Mate Second Class, U.S. Navy,
serving with 2d Battalion, 26th Marines, 5th Marine Division.
Place and date
Iwo Jima, Volcano Islands group, 3 March 1945.

CITATION
For conspicuous gallantry and intrepidity at the risk of his life

above and beyond the call of duty while serving with the 2d Battalion, 26th Marines, 5th Marine Division, during action against enemy Japanese forces on Iwo Jima in the Volcano group on 3 March 1945.

Painfully wounded in the bitter action on 26 February, Wahlen remained on the battlefield, advancing well forward of the frontlines to aid a wounded marine, carrying him back to safety despite a terrific concentration of fire. Tireless in his ministrations, he consistently disregarded all danger to attend his fighting comrades as they fell under the devastating rain of shrapnel and bullets, and rendered prompt assistance to various elements of his combat group as required.

When an adjacent platoon suffered heavy casualties, he defied the continuous pounding of heavy mortars and deadly fire of enemy rifles to care for the wounded, working rapidly in an area swept by constant fire and treating 14 casualties before returning to his own platoon. Wounded again on 2 March, he gallantly refused evacuation, moving out with his company the following day in a furious assault across 600 yards of open terrain and repeatedly rendering medical aid while exposed to the blasting fury of powerful Japanese guns. Stouthearted and indomitable, he persevered in his determined efforts as his unit waged fierce battle and, unable to walk after sustaining a third agonizing wound, resolutely crawled 50 yards to administer first aid to still another fallen fighter.

By his dauntless fortitude and valor, Wahlen served as a constant inspiration and contributed vitally to the high morale of his company during critical phases of this strategically important engagement. His heroic spirit of self-sacrifice in the face of overwhelming enemy fire upheld the highest traditions of the U.S. Naval Service.

Gary G. Wetzel
U.S. Army • Vietnam

"I frequently speak to school children. I like to talk about freedom, the importance of an education, and the meaning of unity. I encourage them to like themselves and remember that, at times, we all have to make sacrifices in life.

"In America, we live in a country where freedom is too often taken for granted. We must never forget that a price was paid and sacrifices were made by our forefathers.

"Frequently I ask youngsters, 'If I were to give you a free candy bar, would you eat it?' Then I explain, 'You know that your education is a free gift, eat it. Take advantage of the opportunity and make the very best of this gift.'

"I also like to talk to young boys and girls about the importance of unity. Our heritage and our freedom is in part due to the unity demonstrated by our forefathers. If we, as Americans, will unite in purpose and effort, in our thoughts and ideas, then we will continue to make America great.

"Kids need to like themselves. You have to like yourself if you are going to be liked by others. I encourage kids to find at least four positive things about themselves and to work on them.

"Finally I remind them that, at times, life is difficult and we have to make personal sacrifices. I also tell them of the importance of service to our nation. Many of life's lessons are learned when you serve others and your nation. By serving, you bless not only others, but you bless yourself."

<hr/>

Rank and organization
Specialist Fourth Class (then Pfc.), U.S. Army,
173d Assault Helicopter Company.
Place and date
Near Ap Dong An, Republic of Vietnam, 8 January 1968.

CITATION

Sp4c. Wetzel, 173d Assault Helicopter Company, distinguished himself by conspicuous gallantry and intrepidity at the risk of his life, above and beyond the call of duty.

Sp4c. Wetzel was serving as door gunner aboard a helicopter which was part of an insertion force trapped in a landing zone by intense and deadly hostile fire. Sp4c. Wetzel was going to the aid of his aircraft commander when he was blown into a rice paddy and critically wounded by 2 enemy rockets that exploded just inches from his location. Although bleeding profusely due to the loss of his left arm and severe wounds in his right arm, chest, and left leg, Sp4c. Wetzel staggered back to his original position in his gun-well and took the enemy forces under fire. His machinegun was the only weapon placing effective fire on the enemy at that time. Through a resolve that overcame the shock and intolerable pain of his injuries, Sp4c. Wetzel remained at his position until he had eliminated the automatic weapons emplacement that had been inflicting heavy casualties on the American troops and preventing them from moving against this strong enemy force.

Refusing to attend his own extensive wounds, he attempted to return to the aid of his aircraft commander but passed out from loss of blood. Regaining consciousness, he persisted in his efforts to drag himself to the aid of his fellow crewman. After an agonizing effort, he came to the side of the crew chief who was attempting to drag the wounded aircraft commander to the safety of a nearby dike. Unswerving in his devotion to his fellow man, Sp4c. Wetzel assisted his crew chief even though he lost consciousness once again during this action.

Sp4c. Wetzel displayed extraordinary heroism in his efforts to aid his fellow crewmen. His gallant actions were in keeping with the highest traditions of the U.S. Army and reflect great credit upon himself and the Armed Forces of his country.

The Long Wait...

Many have had to wait long years before their bravery was acknowledged with the awarding of a Medal of Honor, but perhaps not many so long as Theodore Roosevelt for his valor as a member of the Rough Riders. On July 1, 1898, exposed as the only man on horseback, a target above the rest of the troops on foot, Colonel Theodore Roosevelt displayed uncommon valor as he led charges at Kettle Hill and San Juan Heights during the Battle of San Juan Heights in Cuba.

Those who fought with him, both above and below him in rank, commended him for his bravery and leadership at the head of the Rough Rider unit which he helped to recruit and commanded in battle. He was recommended for the Medal of Honor, an award which he felt very deeply that he deserved. It would not be until more than one hundred years later, however, when he would finally be recognized for his bravery on that day. On January 16, 2001, Theodore Roosevelt became the first President to be awarded the Medal of Honor. His citation reads in part:

Lieutenant Colonel Roosevelt, in total disregard for his personal safety, and accompanied by only four or five men, led a desperate and gallant charge up San Juan Hill, encouraging his troops to continue the assault through withering enemy fire over open countryside. Facing the enemy's heavy fire, he displayed extraordinary bravery throughout the charge, and was the first to reach the enemy trenches, where he quickly killed one of the enemy with his pistol, allowing his men to continue the assault.

He became the only President to ever receive both the Medal of Honor as well as the Nobel Prize for Peace.

Master Sergeant Paul J. Wiedorfer
U.S. Army (Ret.) • WWII

"A few years after I returned home from the war, I was asked to speak at a county fair. The community had banded together to help a widow whose husband had been killed in a farming accident. In a single day, friends and neighbors built a new silo, painted the home and the buildings, put a new roof on the home and strip-cropped the land for the next planting season. It seemed like the entire community rallied together to help out in a time of hardship and need. It was a wonderful demonstration of teamwork and the Golden Rule. I believe it is important to treat others the way you would want to be treated. We should all live by the Golden Rule.

"I would also like to encourage young men and women to make a commitment to both God and country. Commitments are important! My experience as a soldier taught me the truth of the old saying, 'There are no atheists in foxholes.'

"I would also encourage young men and women to continue their education. The greater the level of education you obtain will likely determine the job that you have.

"I also want to stress the importance of honesty. My generation was raised to believe that your word was your bond! For leadership advice I would offer this: Never ask someone to do something that you are not willing to do yourself.

"Finally, I look forward to the day when there will be no living recipients of the Medal of Honor, because, thank God, it will mean that we have learned to live in peace."

———◆◆◆◆◆———

Rank and organization
Staff Sergeant (then Private), U.S. Army,
Company G, 318th Infantry, 80th Infantry Division.
Place and date
Near, Chaumont, Belgium, 25 December 1944.

CITATION

He alone made it possible for his company to advance until its objective was seized. Company G had cleared a wooded area of snipers, and 1 platoon was advancing across an open clearing toward another wood when it was met by heavy machinegun fire from 2 German positions dug in at the edge of the second wood. These positions were flanked by enemy riflemen. The platoon took cover behind a small ridge approximately 40 yards from the enemy position. There was no other available protection and the entire platoon was pinned down by the German fire. It was about noon and the day was clear, but the terrain extremely difficult due to a 3-inch snowfall the night before over ice-covered ground.

Pvt. Wiedorfer, realizing that the platoon advance could not continue until the 2 enemy machinegun nests were destroyed, voluntarily charged alone across the slippery open ground with no protecting cover of any kind. Running in a crouched position, under a hail of enemy fire, he slipped and fell in the snow, but quickly rose and continued forward with the enemy concentrating automatic and small-arms fire on him as he advanced.

Miraculously escaping injury, Pvt. Wiedorfer reached a point some 10 yards from the first machinegun emplacement and hurled a handgrenade into it. With his rifle he killed the remaining Germans, and, without hesitation, wheeled to the right and attacked the second emplacement. One of the enemy was wounded by his fire and the other 6 immediately surrendered.

This heroic action by 1 man enabled the platoon to advance from behind its protecting ridge and continue successfully to reach its objective. A few minutes later, when both the platoon leader and the platoon sergeant were wounded, Pvt. Wiedorfer assumed command of the platoon, leading it forward with inspired energy until the mission was accomplished.

MOH Memorial

The Congressional Medal of Honor Memorial is located in Indianapolis, Indiana. It is the nation's only memorial honoring all recipients of the Medal of Honor.

On the north bank of the Central Canal in White River State Park in downtown Indianapolis, adjacent to Military Park, where the city's first recorded Fourth of July celebration was held in 1822. During the Civil War it was a military camp used for the recruitment and training of troops.

The new memorial was unveiled and dedicated May 28, 1999, the last Memorial Day weekend of the 20th Century.

The memorial features a group of 27 curved glass walls, each between 7-10 feet tall. The walls represent the 15 conflicts, dating back to the Civil War, in which acts of bravery resulted in the awarding of the Medal of Honor. These panels are etched with the names of all the Medal of Honor recipients, their branch of service, and the locations of their heroic actions.

Each day at dusk, a sound system plays 30 minutes of recorded war stories about the medal recipients and their acts of valor. As each story is told, lights illuminate a portion of the memorial to highlight the war or conflict being discussed. Most of the stories have been recorded by living Medal of Honor recipients.

Hershel W. Williams
U.S. Marine Corps • WWII

"No one does anything alone. Even when we are by ourselves, God is there, often only later realized. Two Marines gave their lives that I might live. To God and to them go the credit for my survival. Those of us who served our country and were fortunate to survive, still had and have our duty to perform, which is to LIVE for our country . . .

"All of us live with these words of our heritage: YOU HAVE NEVER LIVED UNTIL YOU HAVE ALMOST DIED...FOR THOSE WHO FIGHT FOR IT, LIFE HAS A FLAVOR THE PROTECTED WILL NEVER KNOW."

Rank and organization
Corporal, U.S. Marine Corps Reserve,
21st Marines, 3d Marine Division.
Place and date
Iwo Jima, Volcano Islands, 23 February 1945.

CITATION

For conspicuous gallantry and intrepidity at the risk of his life above and beyond the call of duty as demolition sergeant serving with the 21st Marines, 3d Marine Division, in action against enemy Japanese forces on Iwo Jima, Volcano Islands, 23 February 1945.

Quick to volunteer his services when our tanks were maneuvering vainly to open a lane for the infantry through the network of reinforced concrete pillboxes, buried mines, and black volcanic sands, Cpl. Williams daringly went forward alone to attempt the reduction of devastating machinegun fire from the unyielding positions. Covered only by 4 riflemen, he fought desperately for 4 hours under terrific enemy small-arms fire and repeatedly returned to his own lines to prepare demolition charges and obtain serviced flamethrowers, struggling back, frequently to the rear of hostile emplacements, to wipe out 1 position after another.

On 1 occasion, he daringly mounted a pillbox to insert the nozzle of his flamethrower through the air vent, killing the occupants and silencing the gun; on another, he grimly charged enemy riflemen who attempted to stop him with bayonets and destroyed them with a burst of flame from his weapon. His unyielding determination and extraordinary heroism in the face of ruthless enemy resistance were directly instrumental in neutralizing one of the most fanatically defended Japanese strong points encountered by his regiment and aided vitally in enabling his company to reach its objective.

Cpl. Williams' aggressive fighting spirit and valiant devotion to duty throughout this fiercely contested action sustain and enhance the highest traditions of the U.S. Naval Service.

Lieutenant Michael E. Thornton
U.S. Navy (Ret) • Vietnam

"My creed or code of conduct for life would include the following:

"Never give up. Hard work and persistence will almost always ensure success. Integrity and character are extremely important and are reflected in the old adage, 'Your word is your bond.' If I offer spiritual advice it would be: Put God first, then country, and both before self. Finally, trust and have faith in God."

Rank and organization
Petty Officer, U.S. Navy, Navy Advisory Group.
Place and date
Republic of Vietnam, 31 October 1972.

CITATION

For conspicuous gallantry and intrepidity at the risk of his life above and beyond the call of duty while participating in a daring operation against enemy forces.

PO Thornton, as Assistant U.S. Navy Advisor, along with a U.S. Navy lieutenant serving as Senior Advisor, accompanied a 3-man Vietnamese Navy SEAL patrol on an intelligence gathering and prisoner capture operation against an enemy-occupied naval river base. Launched from a Vietnamese Navy junk in a rubber boat, the patrol reached land and was continuing on foot toward its objective when it suddenly came under heavy fire from a numerically superior force. The patrol called in naval gunfire support and then engaged the enemy in a fierce firefight, accounting for many enemy casualties before moving back to the waterline to prevent encirclement.

Upon learning that the Senior Advisor had been hit by enemy fire and was believed to be dead, PO Thornton returned through a hail of fire to the lieutenant's last position, quickly disposed of 2 enemy soldiers about to overrun the position, and succeeded in removing the seriously wounded and unconscious Senior Naval Advisor to the water's edge. He then inflated the lieutenant's lifejacket and towed him seaward for approximately 2 hours until picked up by support craft.

By his extraordinary courage and perseverance, PO Thornton was directly responsible for saving the life of his superior officer and enabling the safe extraction of all patrol members, thereby upholding the highest traditions of the U.S. Naval Service.

About the author...

Colonel Jim Coy (Ret.)

Colonel Jim Coy served as a medical consultant for the U.S. Army Special Operations Command. He served two years as the national president of the Special Operations Medical Association and as the national surgeon of the Reserve Officers Association. He lectures both nationally and internationally on combat trauma medicine and his ground-breaking research on lightweight x-ray equipment.

Dr. Coy has served with numerous Special Forces and Special Operations units. He served with the 3rd Group Army Special Forces (AIRBORNE) in the 1991 Gulf War. He has received numerous military honors, awards, and badges that include the Legion of Merit, the Defense Meritorious Service Medal, the Combat Medic Badge, Flight Surgeon Badge, Airborne, Air Assault, and Israeli Airborne Badges. He has also received the Order of Military Medical Merit from the Army Medical Regiment and the prestigious "A" designation—the highest recognition of the Army Medical Department.

He battled with cancer from 1978-1989 with four major surgeries during which portions of his tongue, throat, and jawbone were removed. Today he is considered cured.

Jim and his wife, Vicki, have three children: Tim, Tricia, and Joshua. His family is extremely important to him. He has a vision for men becoming spiritual leaders and standing strong for their families. Colonel Coy is very active in Promise Keepers and Men Without Fear, a local interdenominational group for men, and he is the Men's Ministry director in his home church.

Today, Jim desires to develop a ministry to military and former military men and frequently speaks to community, church, and military groups across the United States.

To contact the author:
COL Jim Coy
www.agatheringofeagles.com
coyjv@socket.net

To contact Family Net to obtain the VALOR video:

Family Net Products
6350 West Freeway
Fort Worth, TX 76116

1-877-FAMNET-7 • 800-832-6638

Other books from Evergreen Press

A Gathering of Eagles–2nd Ed. COL Jim Coy (Ret.)

Three hundred forty-five Medal of Honor recipients, ex-POWs, and leaders in the military, political, and religious arenas share their core beliefs about leadership and success. It demonstrates what makes America great. Photos included of each one.

Among the leaders featured are: Rear Adm. Jeremiah Denton (Ret.), J.C. Watts, Jr., Colin Powell, Billy Graham, James Dobson, Chuck Swindoll, Larry Burkett, Roger Staubach, Gary Smalley, Joseph Stowell, and many more.
ISBN 1-58169-049-5 304 pg. 6 x 9 $14.99

Navigating Toward Home Craig Peters

Provides men with eight breakthrough principles to help them fulfill their responsibilities to their families and have a deeper relationship with the Lord.
• How to set godly priorities and pursue wholesome thinking.
• How to gain spiritual maturity and restore biblical identity.
• Each chapter includes questions for self-evaluation and group discussion.
Endorsed by Todd Blackledge and Dr. Gary Rosberg
ISBN 1-58169-047-9 192 pg. 6 x 8.5 $10.99

So Many Leaders...So Little Leadership Dr. John Stanko

By combining the latest in leadership techniques with a solid biblical foundation, Dr. Stanko delivers cutting-edge tools for leaders who want to build upon their natural abilities and learn how to influence others as servant leaders for the glory of God.

Using Moses, David, and Daniel as examples, the author outlines how to develop a leadership philosophy that includes preparation, perspiration, and inspiration. Great for both up-and-coming leaders and veteran leaders alike.
ISBN 1-58169-048-7 160 pg. 5.25 x 8 $9.99

Faith in the Face of Fear Donald Hilliard, Jr.

A Christian response to the 9-11 attacks, which shows us how to deal with the on-going threats and fears of terrorism
• Shows how to increase faith in the midst of today's uncertainty.
• Includes testimonies of Christians who worked in the twin towers.
• Written by a minister whose people were directly involved in it.
Endorsed by Dr. Mark Chironna and DeForest Soaries, Jr.
ISBN 1-58169-105-X 144 pg. 5.25 x 8 $9.99